AF396012

# An Irish Child's Treasury of Prayers, Blessings and Poems

Gill Books

Hume Avenue, Park West, Dublin 12

www.gillbooks.ie

Gill Books is an imprint of M.H. Gill & Co.

ISBN: 978-1-8045-8199-5

Copyright @ Teapot Press Ltd 2024

This book was created and produced by Teapot Press Ltd

Compilation: Fiona Biggs & Joe Potter
Irish-language editor: Fidelma Ní Ghallchobhair
Illustration: Morena Forza
Design: Tony Potter

Printed in the EU

This book is typeset in Cormorant Infant

The paper used in this book comes from the wood pulp of
sustainably managed forests.



A CIP catalogue record for this book is available
from the British Library.

5 4 3 2 1

# An Irish Child's Treasury of Prayers, Blessings and Poems

Gill Books

# Contents • Ábhar

If one cannot enjoy reading a book over and
over again, there is no use in reading it at all.

*Oscar Wilde*

# INTRODUCTION

This treasury of poems, prayers and blessings for children is designed to be shared by parents with their children, and to be read aloud together. It is arranged thematically, by the months of the year, and will help you and your child to connect with the great gift and wonders of Creation.

January is about new beginnings; February brings with it the first hints of spring and is dedicated to one of our patron saints, Brigid, while March is a full celebration of the season and of our great patron, St Patrick. April is usually the month when we celebrate the greatest feast of all, Easter, and remember the importance of Jesus in our lives. May, the 'month of beauty', a month of new life and joy in nature, is dedicated to Mary, our Mother. June, July and August, when we enjoy long days and short nights, are the carefree months of summer holidays, buckets and spades and lots of outdoor fun. September, with its shorter days and cooler, crisper weather, is back-to-school time. In October we

can feel winter approaching as we shuffle through the autumn leaves that fall to the ground this month, leaving the trees bare for winter. November, with its short days and long nights, makes us appreciate the comforts of home and a nice warm fire. We look forward then to December, which is all about Christmas, friendship, generosity and fun.

You will find here the familiar daily prayers and some that have been tailored to young children as they go about their lives. The poems are a mix of funny rhymes, nature-themed verses and more. Some of them will become familiar to the children as they go through primary school, while others are just fun to read aloud, and many will become firm favourites. Each month has a small offering *as Gaeilge*, including the daily prayers and some poems. This is a book to be dipped into at bedtime, or at any time when you're sitting quietly with your child.

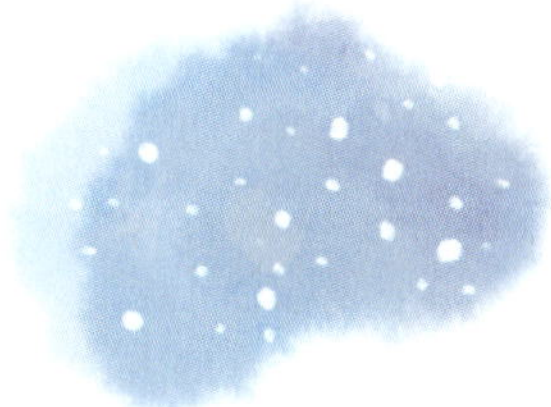

# JANUARY

The New Year has arrived and whether you are glad or sad to say goodbye to the old year, this is the time for new beginnings. As the January frosts blanket the hills and mountains of Ireland, the New Year promises hope of new things to come. With each passing day, January invites children to learn new things about themselves and the world we live in.

Prayers, poems and blessings offer time to reflect at the beginning of a brand new year.

**Prayer**

Dear Lord, thank you for this wonderful New Year.
Fill me with joy and hope in everything I do this year. Amen.

# EANÁIR

**White Fields**

In the winter time we go
Walking in the fields of snow;

Where there is no grass at all;
Where the top of every wall,

Every fence, and every tree,
Is as white as white can be.

Pointing out the way we came,
– Every one of them the same –

All across the fields there be
Prints in silver filigree;

And our mothers always know,
By the footprints in the snow,

Where it is the children go.

*James Stephens*

## A Prayer to Jesus When You Wake Up

Good morning, Lord Jesus,
this day is for you.
Please bless everything I think, say and do.

## Seasons

Ah, Wind, is it Winter?
Yes, Winter is here;
With snow on the meadow,
And ice on the mere.
The daylight is short,
But the firelight is long;
Our skating's good sport;
Then story and song.

*William Allingham (excerpt)*

## Glóir don Athair

Glóir don Athair,
agus don Mhac,
agus don Spiorad Naomh.
Mar a bhí ó thus,
mar atá anois,
Agus mar a bheas go brách,
le saol na saol. Áiméan.

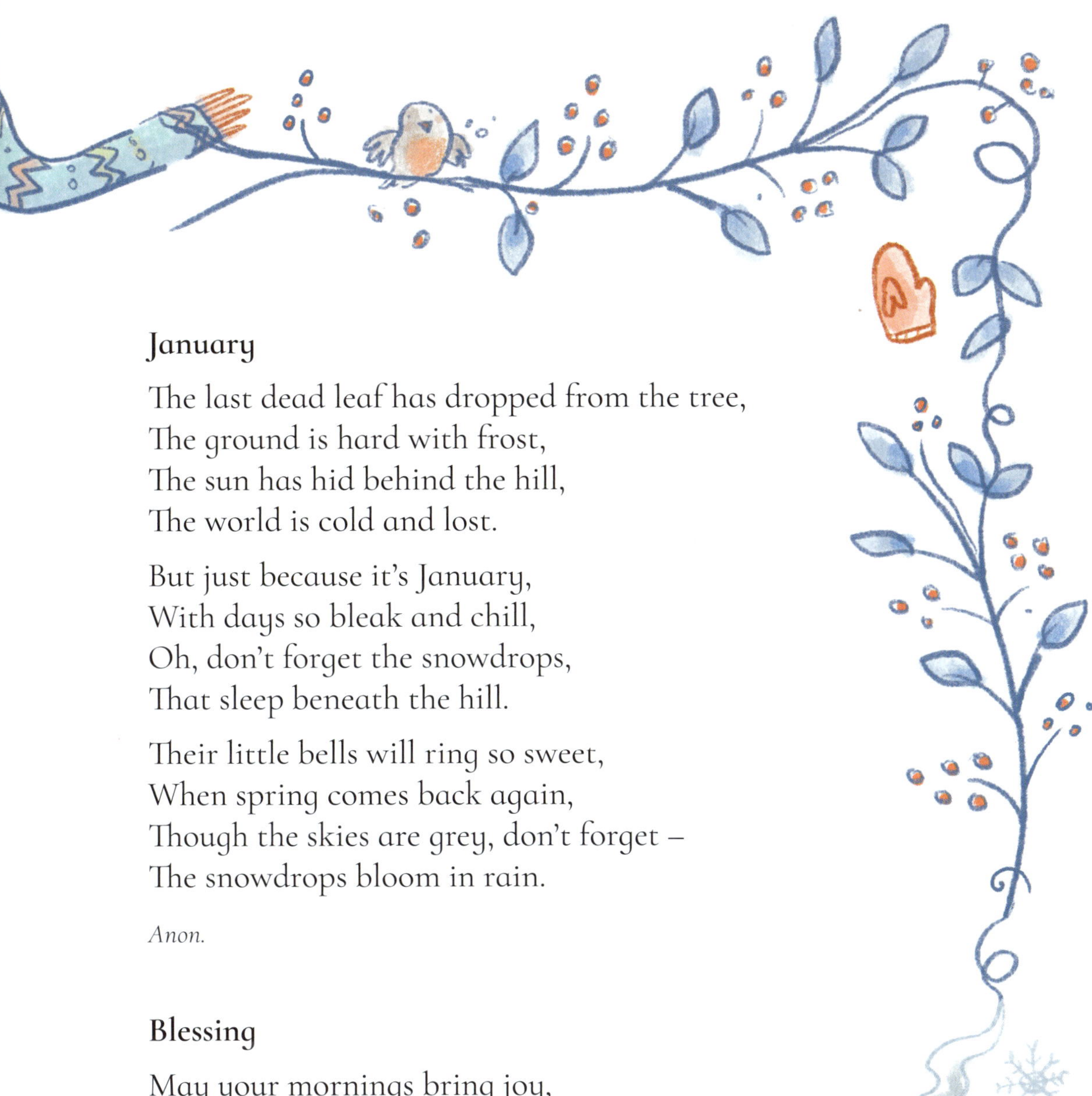

## January

The last dead leaf has dropped from the tree,
The ground is hard with frost,
The sun has hid behind the hill,
The world is cold and lost.

But just because it's January,
With days so bleak and chill,
Oh, don't forget the snowdrops,
That sleep beneath the hill.

Their little bells will ring so sweet,
When spring comes back again,
Though the skies are grey, don't forget –
The snowdrops bloom in rain.

*Anon.*


## Blessing

May your mornings bring joy,
And your evenings bring peace.
May the night be gentle,
And may your rest be sweet.


## A Prayer of Thanks

The sky is ice blue,
The hedges are edged with silver,
The sun bounces light around everything …
Thank you, God, for a lovely day. Amen.

## Morning Prayer to Your Guardian Angel

Angel of God, my guardian dear,
To whom God's love commits me here,
Ever this day, be at my side,
To light and guard,
To rule and guide.
Amen.

## Blessing for Playtime

Bless our games and all our play,
And keep us safe throughout the day.

## Grace before Meals

God is great,
God is good,
Let us thank him for our food.
Amen.

## On Snow – A Riddle

From Heaven I fall, though from earth I begin.
No lady alive can show such a skin.
I'm bright as an angel, and light as a feather,
But heavy and dark, when you squeeze me together.

Though candour and truth in my aspect I bear,
Yet many poor creatures I help to insnare.
Though so much of Heaven appears in my make,
The foulest impressions I easily take.
My parent and I produce one another,
The mother the daughter, the daughter the mother.

*Jonathan Swift*

## Our Father

Our Father,
Who art in heaven,
hallowed be Thy name;
Thy kingdom come;
Thy will be done on earth as it is in heaven.
Give us this day our daily bread;
and forgive us our trespasses as we forgive those
who trespass against us; and lead us not into
temptation, but deliver us from evil.
Amen.

## Towards Winter

The night is cold on the Great Bog.
The storm is lashing – no small matter.
The sharp wind is laughing at the groans
echoing through the cowering wood.

*Anon.*

Psalm 148:7–8

Praise the Lord from the earth, you
sea monsters and all ocean deeps, fire
and hail, snow and frost, stormy wind
fulfilling his command! Mountains and
all hills, fruit trees and all cedars! Wild
animals and all cattle, creeping things
and flying birds!

## A Winter Blessing

May you have a warm coat to wear
Good boots to keep your feet dry
And a warm fire to sit beside.

## A Morning Prayer

Jesus, when I kneel to pray,
Fill my heart with love for you.
And when I meet the coming day,
Guide me in the things I do.
Amen.

## On the Beach at Fontana

Wind whines and whines the shingle,
The crazy pierstakes groan;
A senile sea numbers each single
Slimesilvered stone.
From whining wind and colder
Grey sea I wrap him warm
And touch his trembling fineboned shoulder
And boyish arm.
Around us fear, descending
Darkness of fear above
And in my heart how deep unending
Ache of love!

*James Joyce*

## Hot Toast

Brown toast, white toast,
butter spread on cool toast,
Black toast, scraped toast,
But the best of all is hot toast,
So, Lord ... Three cheers for toast.

*Peter Dixon*


## A Morning Prayer to St Joseph

Dear St Joseph, watch over and protect me this day
as you protected and cared for Jesus.
May the Lord bless us and watch over us.
May the Lord make his face shine upon us
And be gracious to us,
May the Lord look kindly on us and give us peace;
And the blessing of God almighty,
The Father, the Son, and the Holy Spirit,
Be with us and remain with us now and every day.
Amen.

## Praise to God

Praise God from whom
All blessings flow;
Praise him, all creatures
Here below;
Praise him above,
O heavenly host,
Praise Father,
Son and Holy Ghost.

## Glory Be

Glory be to the Father,
and to the Son,
and to the Holy Spirit.
As it was in the beginning, is now,
and ever shall be, world without end.
Amen.

## The Heart of the Wood

My hope and my love,
we will go for a while into the wood,
scattering the dew,
where we will see the trout,
we will see the blackbird on its nest;
the deer and the buck calling,
the little bird that is sweetest
singing on the branches;
the cuckoo on the top of the fresh green;
and death will never come near us
for ever in the sweet wood.

*Augusta, Lady Gregory*

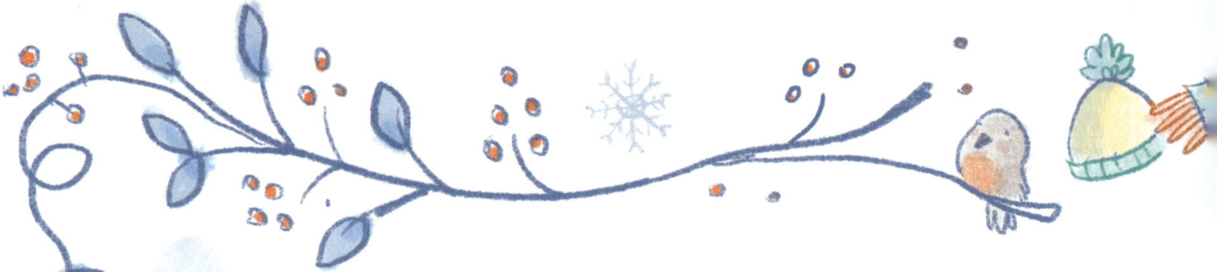

# A Prayer for the Morning

Dear Jesus, thank you for this lovely new day. Help me to appreciate every minute of it until I go to sleep tonight. Amen.

# To A Squirrel At Kyle-Na-No

Come play with me;
Why should you run
Through the shaking tree
As though I'd a gun
To strike you dead?
When all I would do
Is to scratch your head
And let you go.

*W.B. Yeats*

**A Prayer when Lighting the Fire**

I will light my fire today
In the presence of the holy, heavenly angels,
In the presence of Gabriel
Most beautiful form,
In the presence of Uriel of all beauty,
Without hatred, without jealously,
Without fear, without dread of
Anything under the sun,
And with the Holy Son of God as my refuge.
Lord, kindle in my innermost heart
The ember of love
For my enemies, for my relatives,
For my friends,
For the wise, for the foolish, for the wretched.
Amen.

## An Ceol

Mo chroí
Lán leis an gceol
A théann amach
Ón seomra suite
Gach Domhnach ar a seacht a chlog
Nuair a bhíonn an dinnéar críochnaithe

An piano, an fhidil, an fheadóg stáin
Le chéile mar sheanchairde
Is aoibhinn liom na séiseanna
Mo chos ag damhsa faoin mbord
Mo lámha ag cnagadh ar mo ghlúin
Céadfaí líonta

*Sinéad McNally*


## On a Circle

I'm up and down and round about,
Yet all the world can't find me out;
Though hundreds have employ'd their leisure
They never yet could find my measure.
I'm found almost in every garden,
Nay, in the compass of a farthing.
There's neither chariot, coach, nor mill,
Can move an inch except I will.

*Jonathan Swift*

## I am Raftery the Poet

I am Raftery the poet
Full of hope and love
With no light in my eyes
With gentleness that has no misery
Going west upon my pilgrimage
By the light of my heart
Though feeble and tired
To the end of my rove.
Behold me now
With my back to the wall
Playing music
Unto empty pockets.

*Anthony Raftery (Antoine Ó Raifteirí)*


## Job 37:9–10

The tempest comes out from
its chamber, the cold from
the driving winds. The breath
of God produces ice, and the
broad waters become frozen.

### A Prayer of Thanks

For this new morning and its light,
For the rest and shelter of the night,
For health and food, for love and friends,
For every gift your goodness sends,
We thank you, gracious Lord. Amen.

### Psalm 147:16

He spreads the snow like wool
and scatters the frost like ashes.

### Blessing for the Seasons

May each season bring you blessings
And welcome changes in your life.

## The Mystery

I am the wind which breathes upon the sea,
I am the wave of the ocean,
I am the murmur of the billows,
I am the ox of the seven combats,
I am the vulture upon the rocks,
I am the beam of the sun,
I am the fairest of plants,
I am the wild boar in valour,
I am a salmon in the water,
I am a lake in the plain,
I am a word of science,
I am the point of the lance of battle,
I am the God who created in the head the fire.
Who is it who throws light into the meeting on
  the mountain?
Who announces the ages of the moon?
Who teaches the place where couches the sun?
  (If not I)

*Amergin Glúingel (translated by Douglas Hyde)*

## An Evening Prayer

May the Lord support us
   all the day long,
Till the shades lengthen and the
   evening comes,
And the busy world is hushed,
And the fever of life is over,
And our work is done.
Then in his mercy
May he give us a safe lodging,
And holy rest,
And peace at the last. Amen.

*St John Henry Newman*


## Beannacht

Beannacht Dé ort.

## The Forest

Out of the mid-wood's twilight
Into the meadow's dawn,
Ivory-limbed and brown-eyed,
Flashes my Faun!

He skips through the copses singing,
And his shadow dances along,
And I know not which I should follow,
Shadow or song!

O Hunter, snare me his shadow!
O Nightingale, catch me his strain!
Else moonstruck with music and madness
I track him in vain!

*Oscar Wilde*

## Blessing for a Friend Who is Leaving

May the road rise up to meet you,
And may the wind be always at your back.
May the sun shine warm upon your face,
And the rain fall soft upon your fields.
And until we meet again,
May God hold you in the palm of his hand.

# February

February whirls into our lives, bringing the last winds of winter and the first hints of spring. Snowdrops and crocuses push their pretty heads through the frozen soil. We tell ourselves that 'Spring is in the air!' as we look forward to warmer weather and a renewal of nature.

The feast day of St Brigid, one of Ireland's patrons, is on 1 February. We invoke her protection, drawing strength from ancient blessings that have echoed through the ages.

**A Prayer to St Brigid**

Brigid, keeper of the flame, bless us
with your gentle grace,
Guide our steps through winter's
chill, in your warm embrace.
As frosty winds sweep o'er the land,
and darkness claims the day,
We seek your light to lead us on,
along the sacred way. Amen.

 # FEABHRA 

**The Whisper-Whisper Man**

The Whisper-Whisper Man
Makes all the wind in the world.
He has a gown as brown as brown;
His hair is long and curled.
In the stormy winter time
He taps at your window-pane.
And all the night, until it's light,
He whispers through the rain.
If you peeped through a Fairy Ring
You'd see him, little and brown;
You'd hear the beat of his clackety feet
Scampering through the town.

*Anon.*

### A Prayer of Thanks

Thank you, God, for my school each day,
for my teachers who help me to learn and play. Amen.

### Spellbound

The night is darkening round me,
The wild winds coldly blow
But a tyrant spell has bound me
And I cannot, cannot go.
The giant trees are bending
Their bare boughs weighed with snow.
And the storm is fast descending,
And yet I cannot go.
Clouds beyond clouds above me,
Wastes beyond wastes below;
But nothing drear can move me;
I will not, cannot go.

*Emily Brontë*

### Saint Brigid

The dandelion lights its spark
Lest Brigid find the wayside dark,
And brother wind comes rollicking
For joy that she has brought the spring,
Young lambs and little furry folk
Seek shelter underneath her cloak.

*Winifred M. Letts*

## St Brigid's House Blessing

May Brigid bless the house wherein we dwell.
Bless every fireside, every wall and door.
Bless every heart that beats beneath its roof.
Bless every hand that toils to bring it joy.
Bless every foot that walks through its doors.
May Brigid bless the house that shelters us. Amen.

## Blessing of St Brigid's Cross

May the blessing of God, Father, Son and Holy
Spirit be on our Brigid's crosses and on the
places where they hang and on everyone who
looks at them.
Amen.

## Timothy Took His Time

Timothy took his time to school,
And plenty of time he took.
But some he lost at the tadpole pool,
And more at the stickleback brook.
Ever so much at the linnet's nest,
And more at the five-bar gate.
Timothy took his time to school,
But he lost it all and was late.

Timothy has a lot to do –
How shall it all be done?
He didn't get home 'til close on two,
When he might have been home by one.
There's sums and writing and spelling, too,
And an apple tree to climb.
Timothy has a lot to do –
How shall he find the time?

Timothy sought it high and low;
He looked in the tadpole pool
To see if they'd taken the time to grow
That he lost on the way to school.
He found the nest, and he found the tree,
And he found the gate he'd crossed,
But Timothy never shall find (ah me!)
The time that Timothy lost!

*Frida Wolfe*

### A Smile is Like the Sun

A smile is like the morning sun,
It brightens up the day.
It spreads its warmth to everyone,
And chases clouds away.

A smile is like a gentle breeze,
That makes the flowers sway.
It dances through the tallest trees,
And brings joy when we play.

A smile is like a twinkling star,
That sparkles in the night.
It shines no matter where you are,
And fills the dark with light.

So share a smile with all you meet,
And watch it grow and spread.
A simple smile is such a treat,
It's like a hug instead!

*Anon.*

### Ode

We are the music makers,
    And we are the dreamers of dreams,
Wandering by lone sea-breakers,
    And sitting by desolate streams; –
World-losers and world-forsakers,
    On whom the pale moon gleams:
Yet we are the movers and shakers
    Of the world for ever, it seems.

*Arthur O'Shaughnessy*


### A Bedtime Blessing

May God bless you, child.
I put you under the protection of Mary
And her Son,
Under the care of Brigid and her cloak,
And under the shelter of God tonight.


### Beannacht

Beannacht Dé ort.

## The Stolen Child

Where the wandering water gushes
From the hills above Glen-Car,
In pools among the rushes
That scarce could bathe a star,
We seek for slumbering trout
And whispering in their ears
Give them unquiet dreams;
Leaning softly out
From ferns that drop their tears
Over the young streams.
Come away, O human child!
To the waters and the wild
With a faery, hand in hand,
For the world's more full of weeping
    than you can understand.

*W.B. Yeats (excerpt)*

## Antigonish

Yesterday, upon the stair,
I met a man who wasn't there
He wasn't there again today
I wish, I wish he'd go away …
When I came home last night at three
The man was waiting there for me
But when I looked around the hall
I couldn't see him there at all!
Go away, go away, don't you come back any more!
Go away, go away, and please don't slam the door …
  (slam!)
Last night I saw upon the stair
A little man who wasn't there
He wasn't there again today
Oh, how I wish he'd go away …

*Hughes Mearns*

## The Yummy Prayer before Meals

For all food yummy
That fills my tummy,
Thank you, God!
Amen.

## A Morning Prayer

Lord, we thank you for the night
And for the pleasant morning light;
For rest and food and loving care,
And all that makes the day so fair.
Help us to do the things we should,
To be to others kind and good.
In all we do, in work or play,
To grow more loving every day.
Amen.

## Altú tar éis Bia

Go raibh maith agat, a Dhia,
mar is tú a thug bia dúinn.
Go raibh maith agat, a Dhia,
mar is tú a thug cairde dúinn.
Go raibh maith agat, a Dhia,
mar is tú a thug gach rud dúinn.
Go raibh maith agat, a Dhia.
Áiméan.

## Beannacht

Go gcuire Dia an t-ádh ort.

## Good Morning, Jesus

Jesus, you are good and wise
I will praise you when I rise.
Jesus, hear this prayer I send
Bless my family and my friends.
Jesus, help my eyes to see
All the good you send to me.
Jesus, help my ears to hear
Calls for help from far and near.
Amen.

## The Rain

The rain falls gently on the grass,
The rain falls gently down,
It speaks to the flowers and trees,
In a soft and pleasant tone.
In the way that you will show
Jesus, help my hands to do
All things loving, kind and true.
Jesus, guard me through this day
In all I do and all I say.
Amen.

### If I Knew

If I knew the box where smiles were kept,
No matter how large the key
Or strong the bolt, I would try so hard
It would open, I know, for me;
Then over the land and sea broadcast
I'd scatter the smiles to play,
That the children's faces might hold them fast
For many and many a day.

If I knew a box that was large enough
To hold all the frowns I meet,
I would gather them, each and every one,
From nursery, school and street;
Then, folding and holding, I'd pack them in
And turn the monster key,
And hire a giant to drop the box
To the depths of the deep, deep sea.

*Anon.*

## The Beautiful Spring

'I was here first,' said the snowdrop: 'look!'
'Not before me!' sang the silver brook.
'Why,' cried the grass, 'I've been here a week!'
'So have I, dear,' sighed a violet meek.
'Well,' piped a bluebird, 'don't leave me out!
I saw the snow that lay round about.'
'Yes,' chirped a snowbird, 'that may be true;
But I've seen it all the bleak winter through.'
'I came betimes,' sang the south wind, 'I!'
'After me, love!' spake the deep blue sky.
'Who is it cares?' chimed the crickets gay:
'Now you are here, let us hope you'll stay.'
Whispered the sun, 'Lo! the winter's past:
What does it matter who's first or last?
Sky, brooks, and flowers, and birdies that sing,
All help to make up the beautiful spring.'

*George Cooper*


## Song of Solomon 2:11–12

For now the winter is past, the rain is over and gone.
The flowers appear on the earth;
the time of singing has come,
and the voice of the turtledove is heard in our land.

## A Prayer for the Protection of Nature

Dear Father, hear and bless
Thy beasts and singing birds,
And guard with tenderness
Small things that have no words. Amen.


## Kittens! Kittens!

Kittens kittens everywhere
Kittens chewing on my hair
Kittens climbing up my jeans
Kittens hanging from the screens
There's a kitten on each shoulder
Will they do this when they're older?

Kittens fighting on the chairs
Kittens tumbling down the stairs
There's a kitten on my head
There's a kitten in the bread!
There's a kitten in my shoe
I don't believe we just have two!

*Anon.*

### A Seed

See how a Seed, which Autumn flung down,
And through the Winter neglected lay,
Uncoils two little green leaves and two brown,
With tiny root taking hold on the clay
As, lifting and strengthening day by day,
It pushes red branchless, sprouts new leaves,
And cell after cell the Power in it weaves
Out of the storehouse of soil and clime,
To fashion a Tree in due course of time;
Tree with rough bark and boughs' expansion,
Where the Crow can build his mansion,
Or a Man, in some new May,
Lie under whispering leaves and say,
'Are the ills of one's life so very bad
When a Green Tree makes me deliciously glad?'
As I do now.
But where shall I be
When this little Seed is a tall green Tree?

*William Allingham*

## A Prayer of Thanks

Thank you for the world so sweet,
Thank you for the food we eat,
Thank you for the birds that sing,
Thank you, God, for everything.
Amen.


## Pangur Bán

Mise agus Pangur Bán
Ceachtar againn lena shaindán:
Bíonn a mheanma-san le seilg,
Mo mheanma féin i mo cheird.

Nuair a bhímid, scéal gan scís
Inár dteach, sinn araon go haonarach,
Tá cluiche éigríochta againn,
Rud a dtugaimid ár mbeartaíocht dó.

Cé go mbeimis go deimhin ar uaireantaibh
Ní bhodhraímid a chéile:
Is maith le ceachtar a dhán;
Subhaigh gach aon fúthu.

Is é féin máistir dó
Na hoibre a dhéanann sé gach aon lá;
A thabhairt doiraidh do shoiléireacht
Is í m'obair féin.

*Anon. Irish Monk, 9th C (excerpt)*

## Cill Aodáin

Anois teacht an Earraigh beidh an lá dul chun
   síneadh,
Is tar éis na Féil' Bríde ardóidh mé mo sheol.
Ó chuir mé i mo cheann é ní stopfaidh mé choíche
Go seasfaidh mé síos i lár Chontae Mhaigh Eo.

*Antoine Ó Raifteirí (excerpt)*


## The Days of the Month

Thirty days hath September,
April, June, and November;
February has twenty-eight alone.
All the rest have thirty-one,
Except in leap-year – that's the time
When February's days are twenty-nine.

*Anon.*


## Good Memories

Always remember to forget the things
that made you sad, but never forget to
remember the things that made you glad.

## Jesus Bids Us Shine

Jesus bids us shine with a clear, pure light,
Like a little candle burning in the night;
In this world of darkness, we must shine,
You in your small corner, and I in mine.

Jesus bids us shine, first of all for Him;
Well He sees and knows it if our light is dim;
He looks down from heaven, sees us shine,
You in your small corner, and I in mine.

Jesus bids us shine, then, for all around
Many kinds of darkness in this world abound:
Sin, and want, and sorrow – we must shine,
You in your small corner, and I in mine.

Jesus bids us shine, as we work for Him,
Bringing those that wander from the paths of sin;
He will ever help us, if we shine,
You in your small corner, and I in mine.

*Susan B. Warner*

## A Prayer for Every Day

May God the Father keep us safe in his care,
The Lord Jesus Christ be our constant friend,
And the Holy Spirit guide us in all we do.
Amen.

## Blessing

God be with you on your comings and goings,
God be with you on your toings and froings.
God be with you here and God with you there,
With all his grace and loving care.

## A Prayer to the Holy Family

Dear Jesus, Mary and Joseph,
Make our family one with you.
Help us to be instruments of your peace.
May love and grace give us strength
In all the difficult times in our lives.
Amen.

## The Wind and the Moon

Said the Wind to the Moon, 'I will blow you out;
You stare
In the air
Like a ghost in a chair,
Always looking what I am about –
I hate to be watched; I'll blow you out.'

The Wind blew hard, and out went the Moon.
So, deep
On a heap
Of clouds, to sleep,
Down lay the Wind, and slumbered soon,
Muttering low, 'I've done for that Moon.'

He turned in his bed; she was there again!
On high
In the sky,
With her one ghost eye,
The Moon shone white and alive and plain –
Said the Wind, 'I will blow you out again.'

The Wind blew hard, and the Moon grew dim.
'With my sledge
And my wedge
I have knocked off her edge!
If only I blow right fierce and grim,
The creature will soon be dimmer than dim.'

*George MacDonald (excerpt)*

# MARCH

Spring is here! Daffodils crowd the verges, their golden heads bobbing in the breeze. Little lambs frolic in the sunshine. We smile and close our eyes when we begin to feel the warmth of the sun on our faces.

March is the month when we remember St Patrick. Our patron saint, who brought Christianity to Ireland and banished the snakes from our land for ever, is celebrated on 17 March.

Easter moves around, but Lent always falls in March and it often stretches from one end of the month to the other. Although we are celebrating new life, by giving up the things we enjoy, we also remember how Jesus became human to save us.

**St Patrick's Breastplate**

I arise today
Through the strength of heaven;
Light of the sun,
Splendour of fire,
Speed of lightning,
Swiftness of the wind,
Depth of the sea,
Stability of the earth,
Firmness of the rock.

*Attributed to St Patrick (c.8th C)*

# MÁRTA

### Easter Prayer

Come all the faithful, let us worship God,
for through the Cross, joy has come to all the world.
Ever blessing the Lord, we sing his Resurrection,
for having endured the Cross for us,
He has destroyed death by death. Amen.

### A Lent Lily

'Tis the time of Lent, and the lilies grow,
Pure and white as the driven snow.
Buds and blossoms fill the air,
A sign of spring, a time of prayer.

*Christina Rossetti*

### Thank You, God, for Spring

Thank you, God, for spring and the
promise of warmer, longer, brighter days.
Thank you for new growth and life and birth.
Thank you for all the wonderful things
that are waking up in the world. Amen.

### An Irish Spring Blessing

May the raindrops fall lightly on your brow.
May the soft winds freshen your spirit.
May the sunshine brighten your heart.
May the burdens of the day rest lightly upon you.
And may God enfold you in the mantle of His love.

### Beannacht

Go n-éirí an bóthar leat.

### Meditations Divine and Moral

If we had no winter, the spring would
not be so pleasant.

*Anne Bradstreet (excerpt)*

## Daffodils

I wandered lonely as a cloud
That floats on high o'er vales and hills,
When all at once I saw a crowd,
A host, of golden daffodils;
Beside the lake, beneath the trees,
Fluttering and dancing in the breeze.

Continuous as the stars that shine
And twinkle on the milky way,
They stretched in never-ending line
Along the margin of a bay:
Ten thousand saw I at a glance,
Tossing their heads in sprightly dance.

The waves beside them danced; but they
Out-did the sparkling waves in glee:
A poet could not but be gay,
In such a jocund company:
I gazed – and gazed – but little thought
What wealth the show to me had brought:

For oft, when on my couch I lie
In vacant or in pensive mood,
They flash upon that inward eye
Which is the bliss of solitude;
And then my heart with pleasure fills,
And dances with the daffodils.

*William Wordsworth*

## March

Amid the taut gold wires of air the birds
Are feathered shuttles,
Weaving through a warp of twigs
A singing fabric.
Silver and black it is,
A music,
Of thin ebony twigs
And birds' sequin voices.

*Freda Laughton*


## Grace before meals

For every cup and every plateful
Lord, make us truly grateful.

## St Patrick's Breastplate

I arise today, through
God's strength to pilot me:
God's might to uphold me,
God's wisdom to guide me,
God's eye to look before me,
God's ear to hear me,
God's word to speak for me,
God's hand to guard me,
God's way to lie before me,
God's shield to protect me,
God's host to secure me
against snares of devils.

*Attributed to St Patrick (c.8th C)*


## Lúireach Phádraig

Críost liom,
Críost romham,
Críost i mo dhiaidh,
Críost ionam,
Críost ar mo lámh dheas,
Críost ar mo lámh chlé,
Críost i mo chuideachta
Is cuma cá dtéim,
Críost mar chara agam,
Anois is go buan.
Áiméan.

## St Patrick's Breastplate

Christ be with me, Christ within me,
Christ behind me, Christ before me,
Christ beside me, Christ to win me,
Christ to comfort and restore me.
Christ beneath me, Christ above me,
Christ in quiet, Christ in danger,
Christ in hearts of all that love me,
Christ in mouth of friend and stranger.

*Attributed to St Patrick (c.8th C)*


## The Cat and the Moon

The cat went here and there
And the moon spun round like a top,
And the nearest kin of the moon
The creeping cat, looked up.
Black Minnaloushe stared at the moon,
For wander and wail as he would
The pure cold light in the sky
Troubled his animal blood.
Minnaloushe runs in the grass,
Lifting his delicate feet.
Do you dance, Minnaloushe, do you dance?
When two close kindred meet
What better than call a dance?
Maybe the moon may learn,
Tired of that courtly fashion,

A new dance turn.
Minnaloushe creeps through the grass
From moonlit place to place,
The sacred moon overhead
Has taken a new phase.
Does Minnaloushe know that his pupils
Will pass from change to change,
And that from round to crescent,
From crescent to round they range?
Minnaloushe creeps through the grass
Alone, important and wise,
And lifts to the changing moon
His changing eyes.

*W.B. Yeats*

## A Shamrock Blessing

Each petal on the shamrock
Brings a wish your way –
May health, luck and happiness
Be with you every day.

## A Prayer of Thanks for Soap and Water

Dear God, I thank you
For clean water, hot and cold,
For soap, and dry towels.
Amen.


## St. Patrick's Day

A little green on a Sunday,
On a Sunday in the spring,
To bless the dawn of a new day
And the joys that it may bring.

A little green for the Shamrock
That the saint did wear so long,
To show the emerald isle
And her people brave and strong.

The day is full of color,
And the music fills the air,
As we remember Patrick,
And the story he did share.

So let the green be shining
In the sunlight and the rain,
For St. Patrick's Day is here,
With its joy and sweet refrain.

*Katharine Tynan*

## My Shadow

I have a little shadow that goes in and out with me,
And what can be the use of him is more than I can see.
He is very, very like me from the heels up to the head;
And I see him jump before me, when I jump into my bed.

The funniest thing about him is the way he likes to grow –
Not at all like proper children, which is always very slow;
For he sometimes shoots up taller like an india-rubber ball,
And he sometimes gets so little that there's none of him at all.

He hasn't got a notion of how children ought to play,
And can only make a fool of me in every sort of way.
He stays so close beside me, he's a coward, you can see;
I'd think shame to stick to nursie as that shadow sticks to me!

One morning, very early, before the sun was up,
I rose and found the shining dew on every buttercup;
But my lazy little shadow, like an arrant sleepy-head,
Had stayed at home behind me and was fast asleep in bed.

*Robert Louis Stevenson*

## A Prayer for Lent

Dear Jesus,
Thank you for all the good things you give us.
We are sorry that we are not always generous
towards others.
Please help us today to do our best, to be kind and to
help those who need our help.
Amen.

## Prayer to St Joseph

Dear St Joseph,
As Guardian of the Holy Family, you cared for Mary,
and loved Jesus as your own son.
Please protect me and my family,
watching over us and keeping us from harm.
Amen.

### The Fairies

Up the airy mountain,
Down the rushy glen,
We daren't go a-hunting
For fear of little men;
Wee folk, good folk,
Trooping all together;
Green jacket, red cap,
And white owl's feather!
Down along the rocky shore
Some make their home,
They live on crispy pancakes
Of yellow tide-foam;
Some in the reeds
Of the black mountain-lake,
With frogs for their watchdogs,
All night awake.

*William Allingham (extract)*

### Blessing

The peace of God be in your heart.
The grace of God be in your words.
The love of God be in your hands.
The joy of God be in your soul
and in the song that your life sings.


### The Swing

Swinging, swinging,
Swinging high,
Over the fence-post,
Into the sky.

Swinging, swinging,
Down again –
Oh, what joy
To feel the wind and rain!

Swinging, swinging,
Up in the air –
I feel as if
I could swing anywhere!

Swinging, swinging,
Back to the ground –
Oh, the world is a magical place
When you're up and down!

*Annette Wynne*

### The Rainbow

My heart leaps up when I behold
A rainbow in the sky;
So was it when my life began,
So is it now I am a man,
So be it when I shall grow old,
Or let me die!
The child is father of the man;
And I could wish my days to be
Bound each to each by natural piety.

*William Wordsworth*

## A Spring Morning Prayer

Dear Lord, thank you for a fresh start, today and every day.
Thank you for all the wonderful things you have given me.
Help me to let go of all the things that hold me back.
Amen.

## Father William

'You are old, Father William,' the young man said,
'And your hair has become very white;
And yet you incessantly stand on your head –
Do you think, at your age, it is right?'

'In my youth,' Father William replied to his son,
'I feared it might injure the brain;
But now that I'm perfectly sure I have none,
Why, I do it again and again.'

*Lewis Carroll* (from Alice in Wonderland)

**Blessing**

May God bless you with everything you need,
Some of the things that you want,
and all the people that will support and love you.


**Grace Before Meals**

Dear God,
Wherever in the world people break bread together,
May they know the love of Jesus, your son.
Amen.

### I Heard a Bird at Dawn

I heard a bird at dawn
Singing sweetly on a tree,
That the dew was on the lawn,
And the wind was on the lea;
But I didn't listen to him,
For he didn't sing to me.

I didn't listen to him,
For he didn't sing to me
That the dew was on the lawn
And the wind was on the lea;
I was singing at the time
Just as prettily as he.

I was singing all the time,
Just a prettily as he,
About the dew upon the lawn
And the wind upon the lea;
So I didn't listen to him
As he sang upon a tree.

*James Stephens*

## A Thank You Prayer

Thank you for the world so sweet,
Thank you for the food we eat,
Thank you for the birds that sing,
Thank you, God, for everything.
Amen.

## Little Things

Little drops of water,
Little grains of sand,
Make the mighty ocean
And the pleasant land.
Thus the little minutes,
Humble though they be,
Make the mighty ages
Of eternity.

*Ebenezer Cobham Brewer*

## The Lake Isle of Innisfree

I will arise and go now, and go to Innisfree,
And a small cabin build there, of clay and wattles made;
Nine bean-rows will I have there, a hive for the honey-bee,
And live alone in the bee-loud glade.

And I shall have some peace there, for peace comes
dropping slow,
Dropping from the veils of the morning to where the
cricket sings;
There midnight's all a glimmer, and noon a purple glow,
And evening full of the linnet's wings.

I will arise and go now, for always night and day
I hear lake water lapping with low sounds by the shore;
While I stand on the roadway, or on the pavements grey,
I hear it in the deep heart's core.

*W.B. Yeats*

## Mo Mhadra

Ritheann sé
Itheann sé
Suíonn sé
Seasann sé
Imríonn sé
Codlaíonn sé
Siúlann sé
Agus sin é

*Sinéad McNally*

66

## My Treasures

These are treasures that I keep,
I hold them close before I sleep.
A silver coin,
a twisty shell,
a leaf that has a lovely smell,
a birthday badge,
an apple pip,
a very shiny paperclip,
an acorn cup,
a curly straw,
the key to a forgotten door.
These are treasures that I found,
I keep them safe,
I keep them sound.

*Kate Wakeling*


## Prayer before Going to Sleep

Now I lay me down to sleep,
I pray the Lord my soul to keep.
Angels guide me through the night,
and wake me with the morning light.
Amen.

# April

We finally say goodbye to the winds and chills of the first quarter of the year and look forward to enjoying spring. The grass is growing and the blossom is appearing on the trees. We celebrate the wonder of Creation on Earth Day. Easter frequently falls in April and we say goodbye to the restrictions of Lent and celebrate Jesus' resurrection. He conquered death to save us from our sins and give us new life.

**An Easter Blessing**

May the glory and the promise
of this joyous time of year bring
peace and happiness to you and
those you hold most dear.

And may Christ,
Our Risen Saviour,
always be there by your side to
bless you most abundantly
and be your loving guide.

# AIBREÁN

**I Went to the Wood of Flowers**

(No one was with me):
I was there alone for hours.
I was happy as could be
In the Wood of Flowers.
There was grass on the ground,
There were leaves on the trees,
And the wind had a sound
Of such sheer joy,
That I was as happy
As happy could be,
In the Wood of Flowers.

*James Stephens*

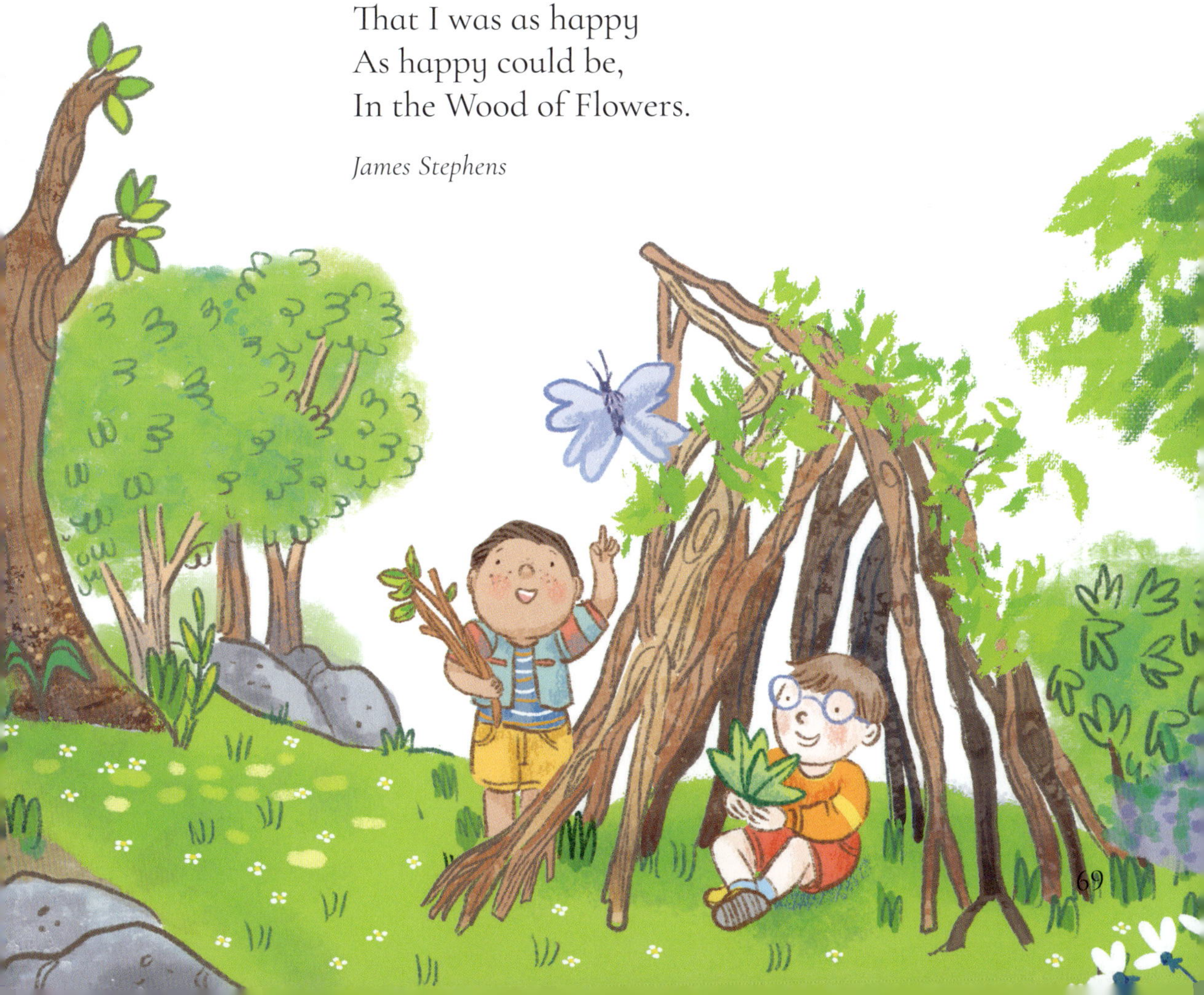

**Morning Prayer**

Into your loving care,
Into your keeping,
You who are everywhere,
Take us, we pray. Amen.

**I Am from Ireland**

I am from Ireland
The holy land
Called Ireland.

Dear friend, please,
Show your generosity,
Come dance with me
In Ireland.

*W.B. Yeats*

## Slow Spring

O year, grow slowly. Exquisite, holy,
The days go on
With almonds showing the pink stars blowing
And birds in the dawn.
Grow slowly, year, like a child that is dear,
Or a lamb that is mild,
By little steps, and by little skips,
Like a lamb or a child.

*Katharine Tynan*


## Prayer

Thank you, God, for spring, with its warmer
days and sunshine and all of the new life we
see around us.
Amen.


## Dhá Éinín Bheaga

Dhá éinín bheaga
Thuas ar an gcrann
Seo é Peadar.
Seo é Seán.

Imigh uaim, a Pheadair,
Imigh uaim, a Sheáin,
Tar ar ais, a Pheadair,
Tar ar ais, a Sheáin.

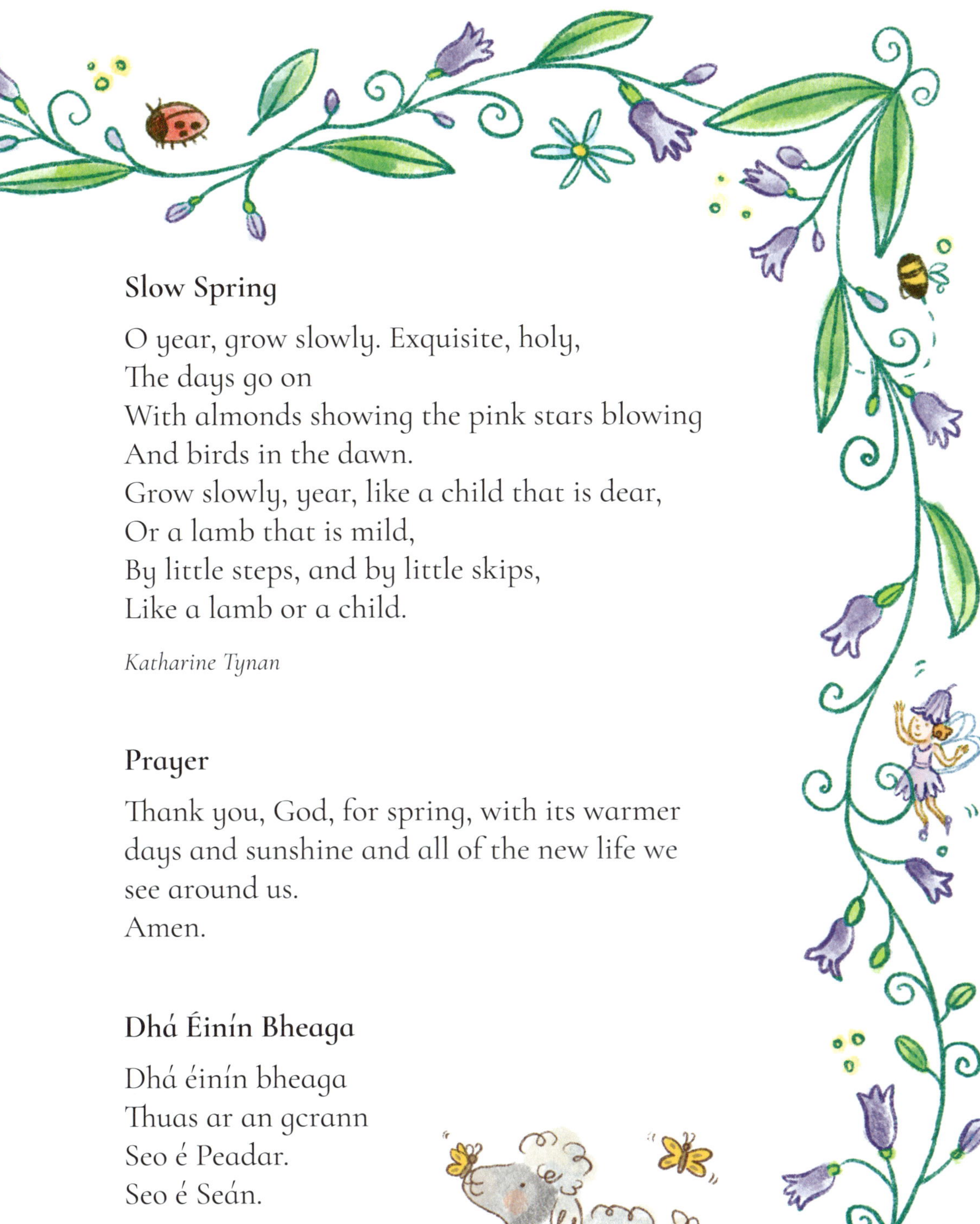

**A Morning Prayer during Lent**

Dear Jesus,
May your light guide my day,
And may your spirit bring me peace. Amen.

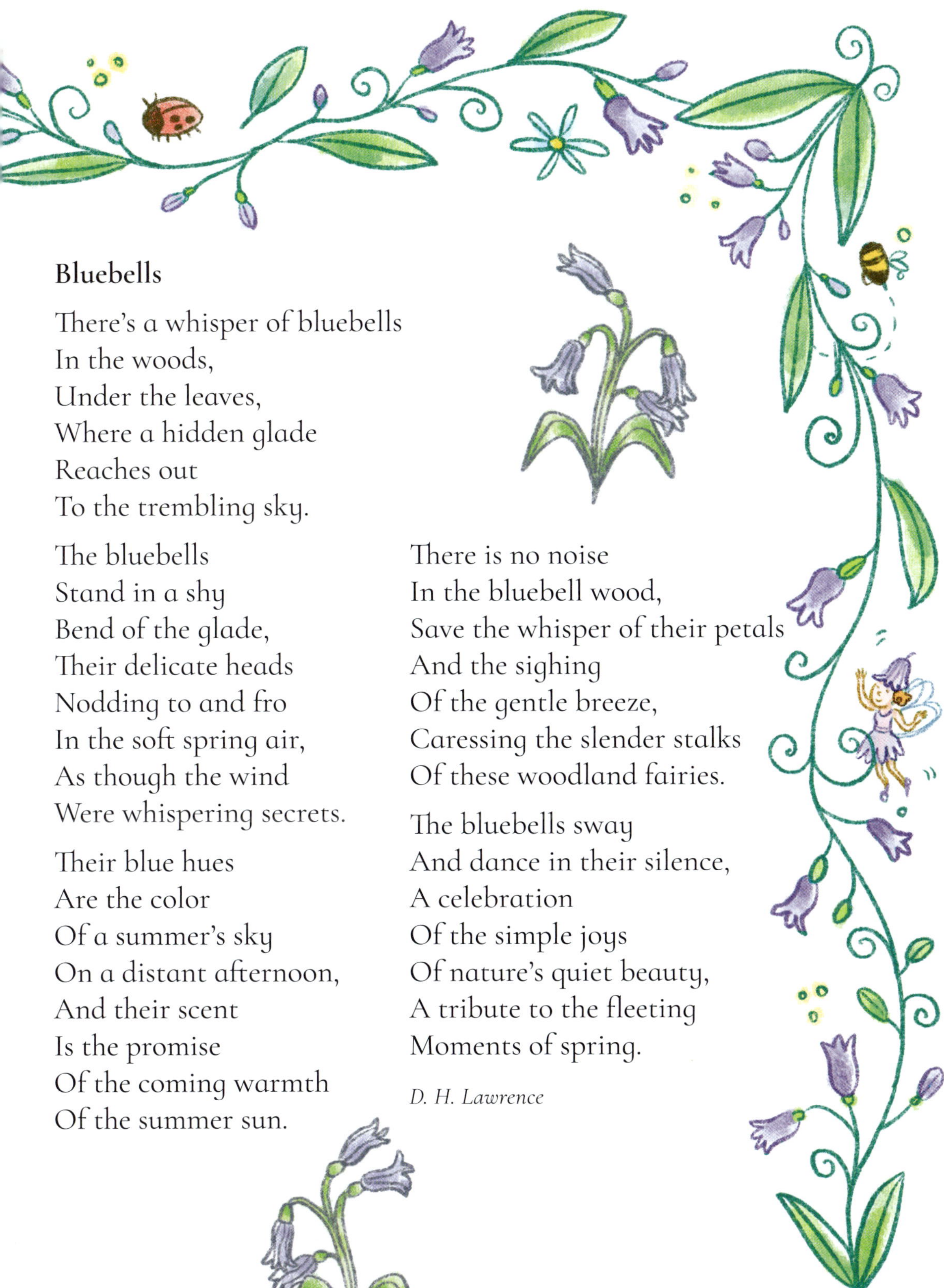

# Bluebells

There's a whisper of bluebells
In the woods,
Under the leaves,
Where a hidden glade
Reaches out
To the trembling sky.

The bluebells
Stand in a shy
Bend of the glade,
Their delicate heads
Nodding to and fro
In the soft spring air,
As though the wind
Were whispering secrets.

Their blue hues
Are the color
Of a summer's sky
On a distant afternoon,
And their scent
Is the promise
Of the coming warmth
Of the summer sun.

There is no noise
In the bluebell wood,
Save the whisper of their petals
And the sighing
Of the gentle breeze,
Caressing the slender stalks
Of these woodland fairies.

The bluebells sway
And dance in their silence,
A celebration
Of the simple joys
Of nature's quiet beauty,
A tribute to the fleeting
Moments of spring.

*D. H. Lawrence*

## All in the April Evening

All in the April evening,
April airs are abroad;
The sheep with their little lambs
Passed me by on the road;
All in the April evening
I thought on the Lamb of God.

The lambs were weary and crying
With a weak human cry,
I thought on the Lamb of God
Going meekly to die.
Up in the blue blue mountains
Dewy pastures are sweet;
Rest for the little bodies,
Rest for the little feet.
But for the Lamb, the Lamb of God
Up on the hilltop green,
Only a cross, a cross of shame,
Two stark crosses between.
All in the April evening,
April airs were abroad;
I saw the sheep with the lambs,
And thought on the Lamb of God.

*Katharine Tynan*

### A Prayer

Dear Jesus,
As the Holy Season of Lent comes to an end, send
the Holy Spirit to open my mind to understand
the greatness of your love for me.
Amen.

### Blessing

May you always feel loved
And know that you are cherished.

## Ár nAthair

Ár nAthair atá ar neamh,
go naofar d'ainm,
go dtaga do ríocht,
go ndéantar do thoil ar an talamh
mar a dhéantar ar neamh.
Ár n-arán laethúil tabhair dúinn inniu,
agus maith dúinn ár bhfiacha
mar a mhaithimidne dár bhféichiúna féin
Agus ná lig sinn i gcathú,
ach saor sinn ó olc.
Áiméan.

## I Watched a Blackbird

I watched a blackbird on a budding sycamore
One Easter Day, when sap was stirring twigs to the core;
I saw his tongue, and crocus-coloured bill
Parting and closing as he turned his trill;
Then he flew down, seized on a stem of hay,
An upped to where his building scheme was under way,
As if so sure a nest was never shaped on spray.

*Thomas Hardy*

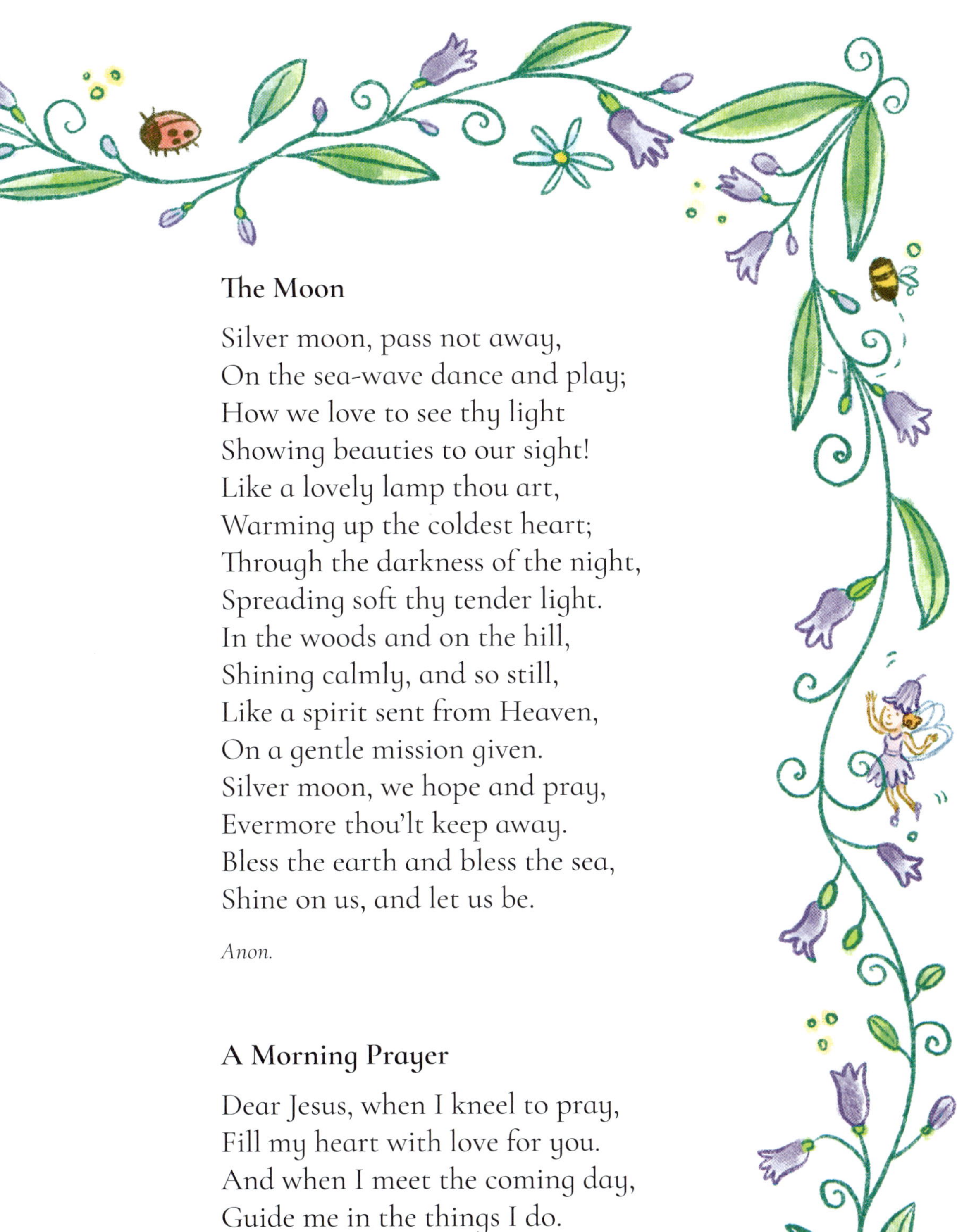

## The Moon

Silver moon, pass not away,
On the sea-wave dance and play;
How we love to see thy light
Showing beauties to our sight!
Like a lovely lamp thou art,
Warming up the coldest heart;
Through the darkness of the night,
Spreading soft thy tender light.
In the woods and on the hill,
Shining calmly, and so still,
Like a spirit sent from Heaven,
On a gentle mission given.
Silver moon, we hope and pray,
Evermore thou'lt keep away.
Bless the earth and bless the sea,
Shine on us, and let us be.

*Anon.*


## A Morning Prayer

Dear Jesus, when I kneel to pray,
Fill my heart with love for you.
And when I meet the coming day,
Guide me in the things I do.
Amen.

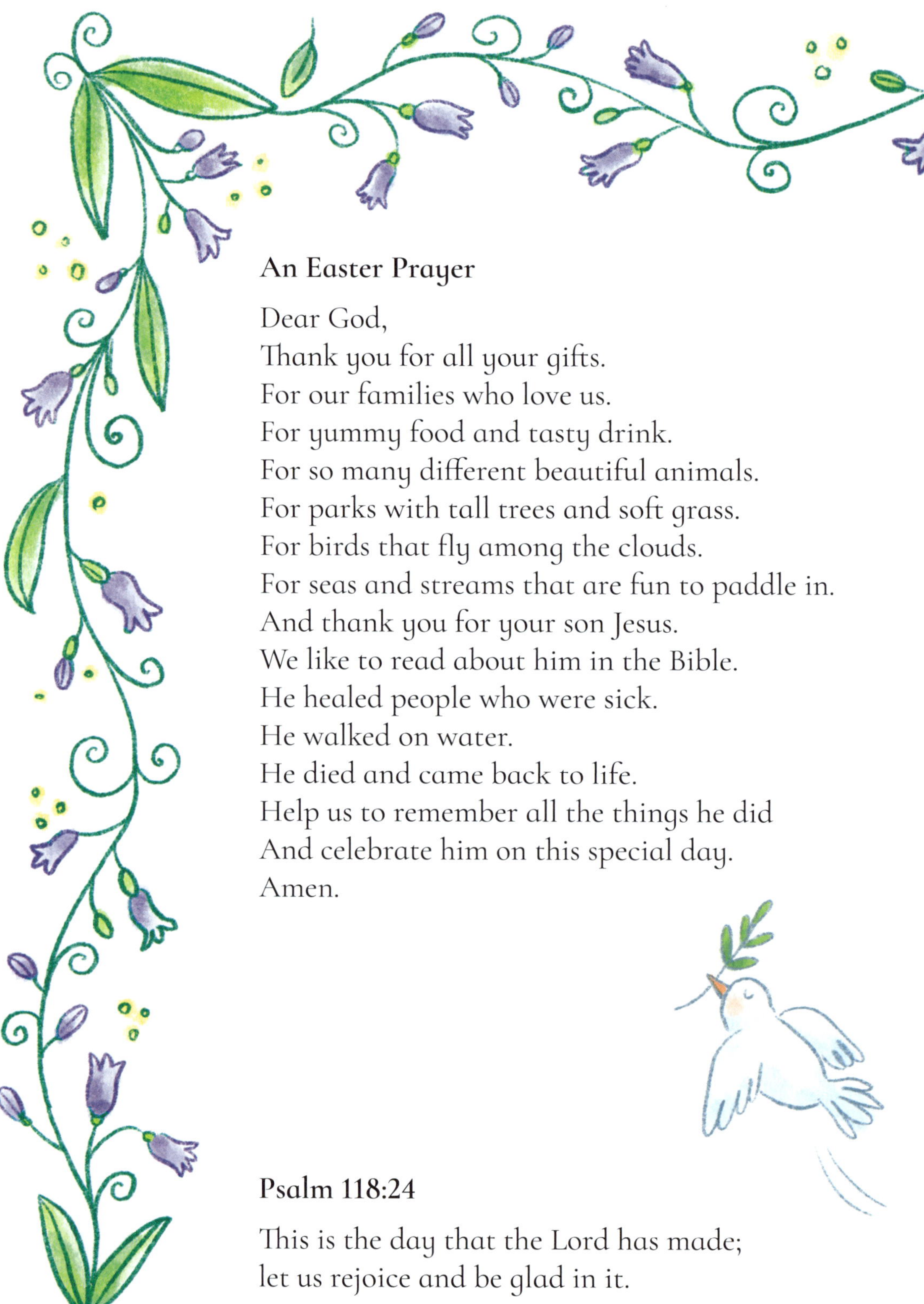

**An Easter Prayer**

Dear God,
Thank you for all your gifts.
For our families who love us.
For yummy food and tasty drink.
For so many different beautiful animals.
For parks with tall trees and soft grass.
For birds that fly among the clouds.
For seas and streams that are fun to paddle in.
And thank you for your son Jesus.
We like to read about him in the Bible.
He healed people who were sick.
He walked on water.
He died and came back to life.
Help us to remember all the things he did
And celebrate him on this special day.
Amen.

**Psalm 118:24**

This is the day that the Lord has made;
let us rejoice and be glad in it.

## The Easter Flower

Far from this foreign Easter
Damp and chilly
My soul steals to a pear-shaped
Plot of ground,
Where gleamed the
Lilac-tinted lily
Soft-scented in the air for yards around;
Alone, without a hint of guardian leaf!
Just like a fragile bell of silver rime,
It burst the tomb for freedom sweet and brief
In the young pregnant year at Eastertime;
And many thought it was a sacred sign,
And some called it the resurrection flower;
And I, a pagan, worshipped at its shrine,
Yielding my heart unto its perfumed power.

*Claude McKay*

**An Easter Blessing**

May the glory
and the promise
of this joyful time of year
bring peace
and happiness to you
and those you hold dear.

**Easter Eggs**

Yellow and blue.
Easter eggs,
For me and you
Easter eggs,
Candy sweet.
Easter eggs
Are good to eat.
Easter eggs,
Pretty and funny.
But ... where, oh where
Is the Easter bunny?

*Anon.*

## An Easter Carol

Spring bursts to-day,
For Christ is risen and all the earth's at play.

Flash forth, thou Sun,
The rain is over and gone, its work is done.

Winter is past,
Sweet Spring is come at last, is come at last.

Bud, Fig and Vine,
Bud, Olive, fat with fruit and oil and wine.

Break forth this morn
In roses, thou but yesterday a Thorn.

Uplift thy head,
O pure white Lily through the Winter dead.

Sing, Creatures, sing,
Angels and Men and Birds and everything.

*Christina Rossetti*

## A Morning Prayer

For this new morning and its light,
For the rest and shelter of the night,
For health and food, for love and friends,
For every gift your goodness sends,
We thank you, gracious Lord.
Amen.


## Four Ducks on a Pond

Four ducks on a pond,
A grass-bank beyond,
A blue sky of spring,
White clouds on the wing;
What a little thing
To remember for years –
To remember with tears!

*William Allingham*

## Springtime Prayer

For flowers that bloom about our feet,
For tender grass, so fresh, so sweet,
For song of bird, and hum of bee,
For all things fair we hear or see,
Father in heaven, we thank Thee!
For blue of stream and blue of sky,
For pleasant shade of branches high,
For fragrant air and cooling breeze,
For beauty of the blooming trees,
Father in heaven, we thank Thee!

*Ralph Waldo Emerson*

**Beannacht**

Go ndéana an t-ádh ar do thuras.


**The Rain**

Rain on the green grass,
And rain on the tree,
And rain on the house top,
But not on me!
*Anon.*

## Bird Thoughts

I lived first in a little house,
And lived there very well;
I thought the world was small and round,
And made of pale blue shell.

I lived next in a little nest,
Nor needed any other;
I thought the world was made of straw,
And brooded by my mother.

One day I fluttered from the nest
To see what I could find.
I said, 'The world is made of leaves;
I have been very blind.'

At length I flew beyond the tree,
Quite fit for grown-up labours.
I don't know how the world is made,
And neither do my neighbours!

*Anon.*

**A Prayer of Thanks**

Dear God,
Thank you for spring and the promise of
brighter, sunnier days after a long winter.
Thank you for all the new life we see
around us.
Amen.


**Blessing**

May your troubles be less
And your blessings be more
And may nothing but happiness
Come through your door.

## The Thrush

When Winter's ahead,
What can you read in November
That you read in April
When Winter's dead?
I hear the thrush, and I see
Him alone at the end of the lane
Near the bare poplar's tip,
Singing continuously.

*Edward Thomas*


## April Rain

Rain, rain go away
Come again another day
Little Baby wants to play
Rain, rain go away

Rain, rain go away
Come again another day
Everybody wants to play
Rain, rain go away.

*Anon.*

# MAY

Winter is finally at an end, summer is waiting around the corner, the flowers are blooming and the butterflies and bees are hard at work in our gardens and out in the countryside. The grain is ripening in the fields, promising a good harvest.

Some children will make their First Holy Communion in May, usually when they are around seven or eight years old.

May is said to be the 'month of beauty', and now that nature is at its freshest and most beautiful, we give thanks for all the good things we enjoy at this time of year.

## A Bird is Calling from the Willow

A bird is calling from the willow
with lovely beak, a clean call.
Sweet yellow tip; he is black and strong.
He is doing a dance, the blackbird's song.

*Anon.*

# BEALTAINE

## May Day

A delicate fabric of bird song
Floats in the air,
The smell of wet wild earth
Is everywhere.
Red small leaves of the maple
Are clenched like a hand,
Like girls at their first communion
The pear trees stand.
Oh I must pass nothing by
Without loving it much,
The raindrop try with my lips,
The grass with my touch;
For how can I be sure
I shall see again
The world on the first of May
Shining after the rain?

*Sara Teasdale*

### Hail Mary

Hail Mary, Full of Grace, The Lord is with thee.
Blessed art thou among women, and blessed is
the fruit of thy womb, Jesus.

Holy Mary, Mother of God,
pray for us sinners now,
and at the hour of our death.
Amen.

### Blessing

May you remember,
Every morning when you wake up,
And every night when you go to sleep,
That you are loved.

**Bring Flowers of the Fairest**

Bring flowers of the fairest,
Bring flowers of the rarest,
From garden and woodland and hillside and dale;
Our full hearts are swelling,
Our glad voices telling
The praise of the loveliest flower of the vale!
O Mary, we crown you with blossoms today!
Queen of the Angels, Queen of the May.
O Mary, we crown you with blossoms today,
Queen of the Angels, Queen of the May.

*Mary E. Walsh*

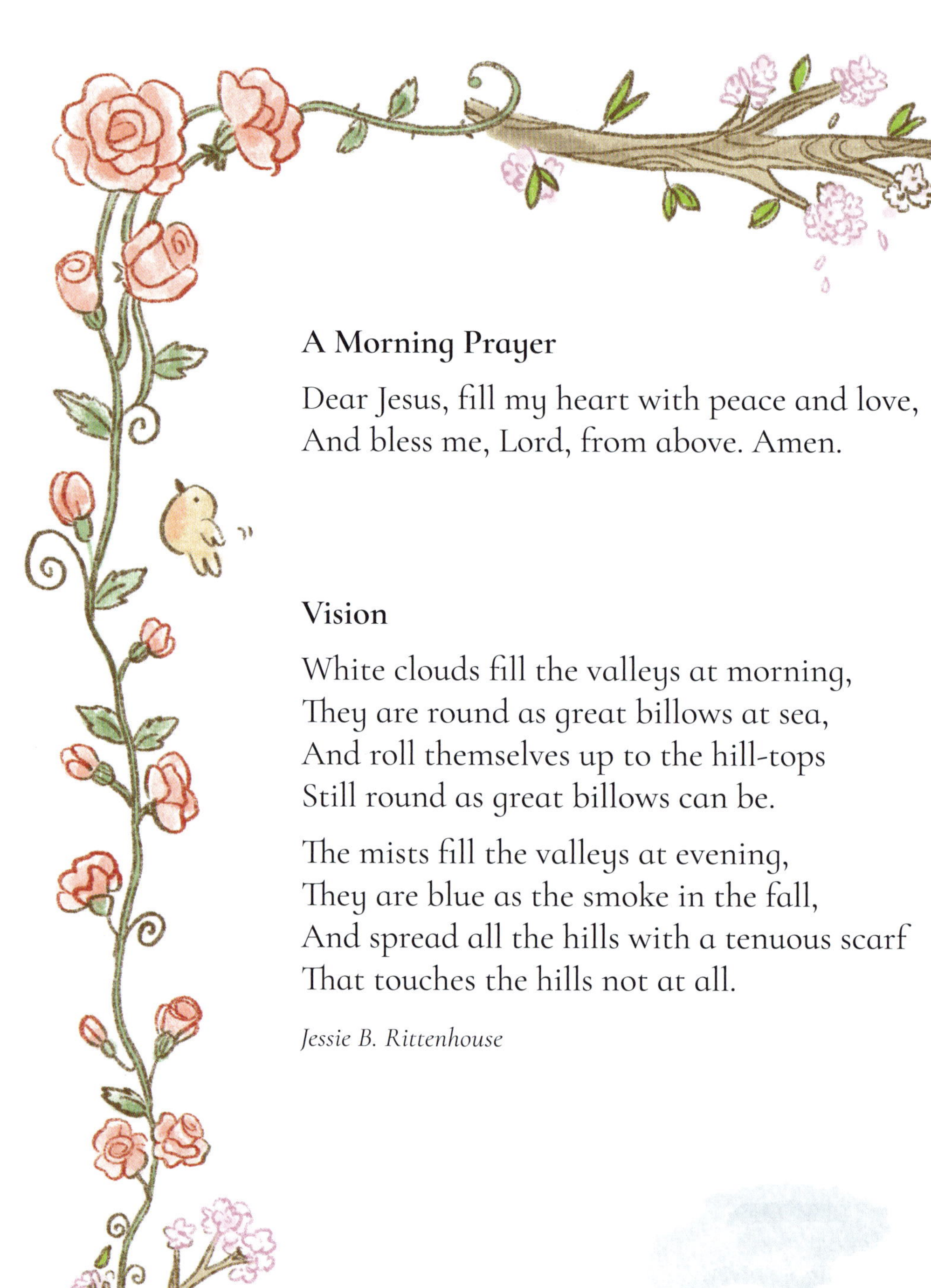

## A Morning Prayer

Dear Jesus, fill my heart with peace and love,
And bless me, Lord, from above. Amen.


## Vision

White clouds fill the valleys at morning,
They are round as great billows at sea,
And roll themselves up to the hill-tops
Still round as great billows can be.

The mists fill the valleys at evening,
They are blue as the smoke in the fall,
And spread all the hills with a tenuous scarf
That touches the hills not at all.

*Jessie B. Rittenhouse*

## Blessing

May Mary, the Mother of God, come
into your life today with a special blessing for you.

## To Our Lady

Lovely Lady dressed in blue –
Teach me how to pray!
God was just your little boy,
Tell me what to say!

Did you lift Him up, sometimes,
Gently on your knee?
Did you sing to Him the way
Mother does to me?

Did you hold His hand at night?
Did you ever try
Telling stories of the world?
O! And did He cry?

Do you really think He cares
If I tell Him things –
Little things that happen? And
Do the Angels' wings

Make a noise? And can He hear
Me if I speak low?
Does He understand me now?
Tell me – for you know.

Lovely Lady dressed in blue –
Teach me how to pray!
God was just your little boy,
And you know the way.

*Mary Dixon Thayer*

## A Prayer to Mary

Dear Mary, my mother,
Help me to be what you want me to be.
Take my hand in yours so I can always
   be with you.
Amen.


## Beannacht le haghaidh Mhí na Bealtaine

Go dtuga Dia solas do shúil,
sonas do chroí, agus éadaí glan
do chorp, ar feadh mhí na Bealtaine.
Go maire tú i gcéad aoibhinn éachtaí!

## An Magnificat

Mórann m'anam an Tiarna,
agus rinne mo spiorad gairdeas i nDia, mo
  shlánaitheoir;
Óir dhearc sé le fabhar ar ísle a bhanóglaigh,
Mar féach, déarfaidh na glúine uile feasta gur méanar
  dom.
Áiméan.

## A Morning Prayer to Mary

Holy Mary, our mother,
Filled with love for God,
Pray for us today.
Amen.

## Check

The night was creeping on the ground;
She crept and did not make a sound
Until she reached the tree, and then
She covered it, and stole again
Along the grass beside the wall.

I heard the rustle of her shawl
As she threw blackness everywhere
Upon the sky and ground and air,
And in the room where I was hid:
But no matter what she did
To everything that was without,
She could not put my candle out.

So I stared at the night, and she
Stared back solemnly at me.

*James Stephens*

## A Prayer to Mary

Dear Mary, you were always ready to look after people who needed you. Please help me to be like you and look after all those people who need my help.
Amen.

## The Eagle

He clasps the crag with crooked hands;
Close to the sun in lonely lands,
Ringed with the azure world, he stands.

The wrinkled sea beneath him crawls;
He watches from his mountain walls,
And like a thunderbolt he falls.

*Alfred Lord Tennyson*

## Have You Ever Seen?

Have you ever seen a sheet on a river bed?
Or a single hair from a hammer's head?
Has the foot of a mountain any toes?
And is there a pair of garden hose?

Does the needle ever wink its eye?
Why doesn't the wing of a building fly?
Can you tickle the ribs of a parasol?
Or open the trunk of a tree at all?

Are the teeth of a rake ever going to bite?
Have the hands of a clock any left or right?
Can the garden plot be deep and dark?
And what is the sound of the birch's bark?

*Anon.*

## Music

It's the finest music in the land.
Sung by a choir, that's not very grand.
The one you can hear singing top note,
Is a Black and White Billy or Mountain Goat.
No one reads music, that's not of much use.
Conducting is usually done by the Goose.
The Chickens and Ducks Keep well in Tune,
Our Farm Dog howls by the light of the moon.
The Cows you know start off with a moo,
That's the signal for the Owls too-whit and too-who.
The Sow with her Piglets, begins to grunt.
The Fox joins in and leaves the Hunt.
The Horses are good and give a loud neigh,
Not to be left out the Donkeys bray.
I've not mentioned the Birds of the air,
Wonderful how they all do their share.
The Cats of course are masters of this art,
And with their Kittens all take part.
The Cockerel is perhaps a little too loud,
But then again he is rather proud.
This choir of mine is very well trained,
Only the Church has of yet complained.
We sing our praises to Him on high,
The Poor Old Vicar, can only sigh.
His congregation consists of but few,
I'll help with my choir, how about YOU?

*Annette Wynne*

**Let Dogs Delight to Bark and Bite**

Let dogs delight to bark and bite,
For God hath made them so;
Let bears and lions growl and fight,
For 'tis their nature too.

But, children, you should never let
Such angry passions rise;
Your little hands were never made
To tear each other's eyes.

*Isaac Watts*


**Secret**

We have a secret
Just we three
The robin and I
And the sweet cherry tree.
The robin told the tree
And the tree told me
And nobody knows it
But just we three.

*Anon.*

**A Prayer to Mary**

Holy Mary, my mother,
Filled with love for God,
Pray for us in all our needs.
Amen.


**The Rainbow**

Soft falls the shower, the thunders cease!
And see the messenger of peace
Illumes the eastern skies;
Blest sign of firm unchanging love!
While others seek the cause to prove,
That bids thy beauties rise.

My soul, content with humbler views,
Well pleased admires thy varied hues,
And can with joy behold
Thy beauteous form, and wondering gaze
Enraptured on thy mingled rays
Of purple, green, and gold.

*Charlotte Richardson*

## Blessing

Dear Lord, at the beginning of summer,
when the sun is shining and the birds
are singing, we bless your name.

## Two Legs for Birds

2 legs for birds,
and you and me.
4 legs for dogs,
and squirrels in a tree.
6 legs for beetles.
Away they go!
8 legs for spiders.
What do you know!

*Anon.*

### Old Noah's Ark

Old Noah once he built an ark,
And patched it up with hickory bark.
He anchored it to a great big rock,
And then he began to load his stock.
The animals went in one by one,
The elephant chewing a carraway bun.
The animals went in two by two,
The crocodile and the kangaroo.
The animals went in three by three,
The tall giraffe and the tiny flea.
The animals went in four by four,
The hippotamus got stuck in the door.
The animals went in five by five,
The bees mistook the bear for a hive.
The animals went in six by six,
The monkey was up to his usual tricks.
The animals went in seven by seven,
The cats raising their eyes to heaven.
The animals went in eight by eight,
Some were early and some were late.
The animals went in nine by nine,
They all formed pairs and marched in line.
The animals went in ten by ten,
If you want any more you can read it again!

*Anon.*

## A Prayer of Thanks

Dear Lord who made the birds of the air,
the animals in the field and the birds that
sing, we thank you for the wonderful gift of
nature. Amen.


## Heaven is not Reached at a Single Bound

Heaven is not reached at a single bound,
But we build the ladder by which we rise
From the lowly earth to the vaulted skies,
And we mount to its summit round by round.

I count this thing to be grandly true:
That a noble deed is a step toward God, –
Lifting the soul from the common clod
To a purer air and a broader view.

*J.G. Holland*


## Psalm 23:1–3

The Lord is my shepherd, I shall not want.
He makes me lie down in green pastures;
he leads me beside still waters;
he restores my soul.

## Caint

Tá cigire cainte i mo cheann
A chíorann gach smaoineamh a ritheann tríd,
Ag meá gach focail, ag blaiseadh na bhfonn,
Ag ceilt rún nó fírinne lom,
Ag scagadh freagraí,
Ag baint, ag scrios,
Ag iarraidh frásaí borba a chosc,
Is é is toradh ar a dhianscrúdú
Mo theanga a cheangailt ina snaidhm, ina lúb,
Gach focal stadach,
Frogach, bacach,
Do m'fhágáil balbh i mo Thost.

*Éamonn Ó Ruanaí*

## A Prayer of Thanks

Thank you, Lord, for this new day.
Guide me in your loving way.
Amen.

## Blessing

Bless our hands as
    we create,
Let beauty be in
    all we make.

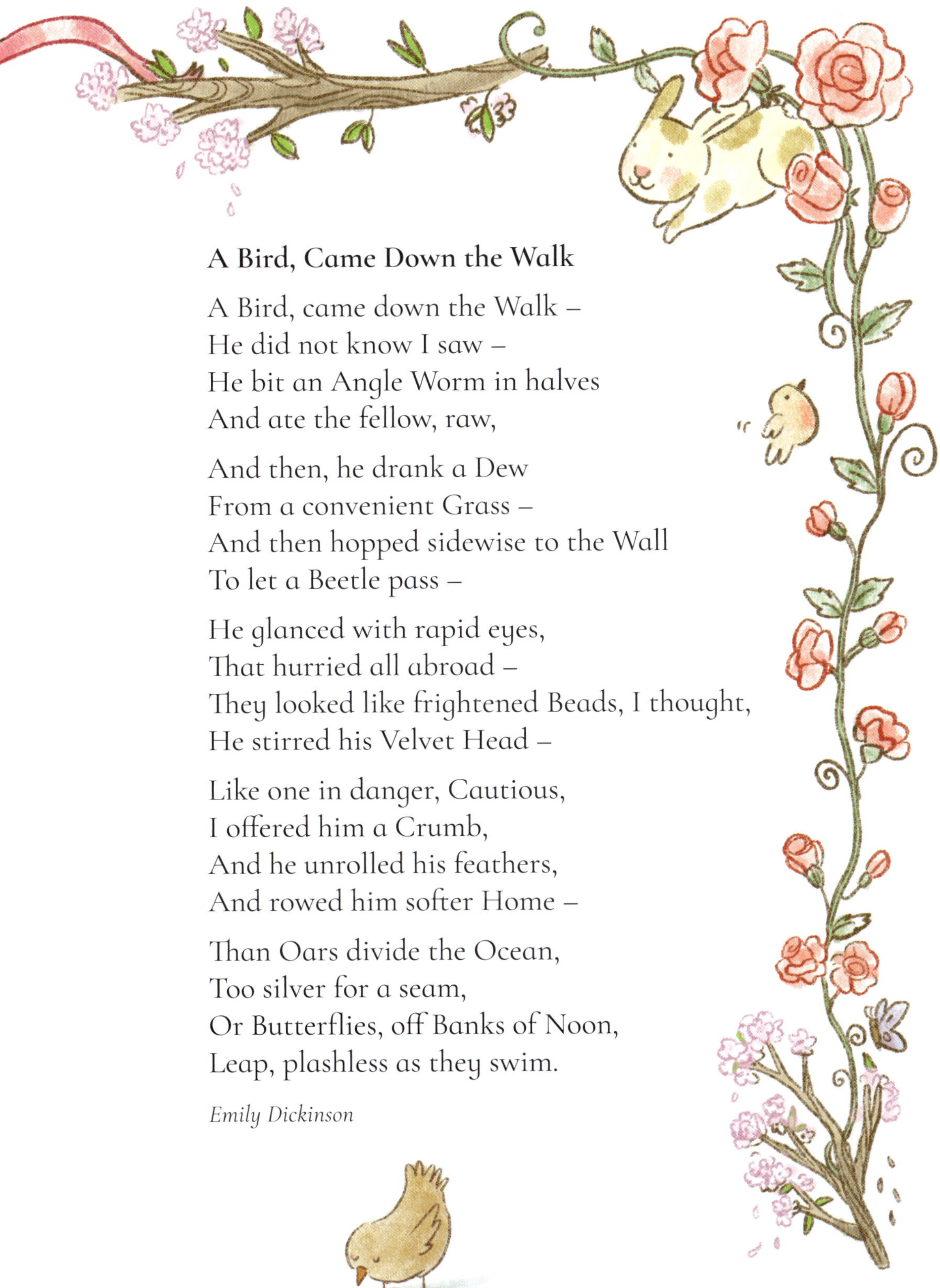

## A Bird, Came Down the Walk

A Bird, came down the Walk –
He did not know I saw –
He bit an Angle Worm in halves
And ate the fellow, raw,

And then, he drank a Dew
From a convenient Grass –
And then hopped sidewise to the Wall
To let a Beetle pass –

He glanced with rapid eyes,
That hurried all abroad –
They looked like frightened Beads, I thought,
He stirred his Velvet Head –

Like one in danger, Cautious,
I offered him a Crumb,
And he unrolled his feathers,
And rowed him softer Home –

Than Oars divide the Ocean,
Too silver for a seam,
Or Butterflies, off Banks of Noon,
Leap, plashless as they swim.

*Emily Dickinson*

# JUNE

A few sunny days make us hope for sunshine and blue skies all summer long. The school holidays are about to begin and we can look forward to weeks of freedom. The world is still wearing its bright green spring-into-summer cloak, the flowers are blooming and the birds are singing in the trees.

In June we can spend long days outside, playing with our friends and going to the beach. We should take the time to look around us at the beautiful world we live in. The feast of St Columba (or Colmcille), one of the three patron saints of Ireland and a lover of animals and nature, is in June.

**Beannacht Mí an Mheithimh**

Go raibh laethanta geala agus sona agat,
go dtuga Dia sláinte duit agus do do theaghlach,
agus go gcuire tú spraoi agus gáire
i ngach lá de mhí an Mheithimh.

# MEITHEAMH

**All Things Bright and Beautiful**

All things bright and beautiful,
All creatures great and small,
All things wise and wonderful,
The Lord God made them all.

Each little flower that opens,
Each little bird that sings,
He made their glowing colours,
He made their tiny wings.

He gave us eyes to see them,
And lips that we might tell,
How great is God Almighty,
Who has made all things well.

The cold wind in the winter,
The pleasant summer sun,
The ripe fruits in the garden,
He made them every one.

All things bright and beautiful,
All creatures great and small,
All things wise and wonderful,
The Lord God made them all.

*Cecil Frances Alexander*

## A Prayer of Thanks

Father, we thank you for the night,
And for the pleasant morning light,
For the rest and loving care,
And all that makes the world more fair.

Help us do the things we should,
To be to others kind and good,
In all we do, in all we say,
To grow more loving every day.
Amen.

## I Have a Little Frog

I have a little frog
His name is Tiny Tim,
I put him in the bathtub,
To see if he could swim,
He drank up all the water,
And gobbled up the soap!
And when he tried to talk
He had a BUBBLE in his throat!

*Anon.*

## The Little Elf-man

I met a little Elf-man, once,
Down where the lilies blow.
I asked him why he was so small,
And why he didn't grow.

He slightly frowned, and with his eye
He looked me through and through.
'I'm just as big for me,' said he,
'As you are big for you.'

*John Kendrick Bangs*

## Blessing

At the first light of sun:
God we bless you.
When the long day is done:
God we bless you.
In our smiles and in our tears:
God we bless you.
Through each day of our years:
God we bless you.

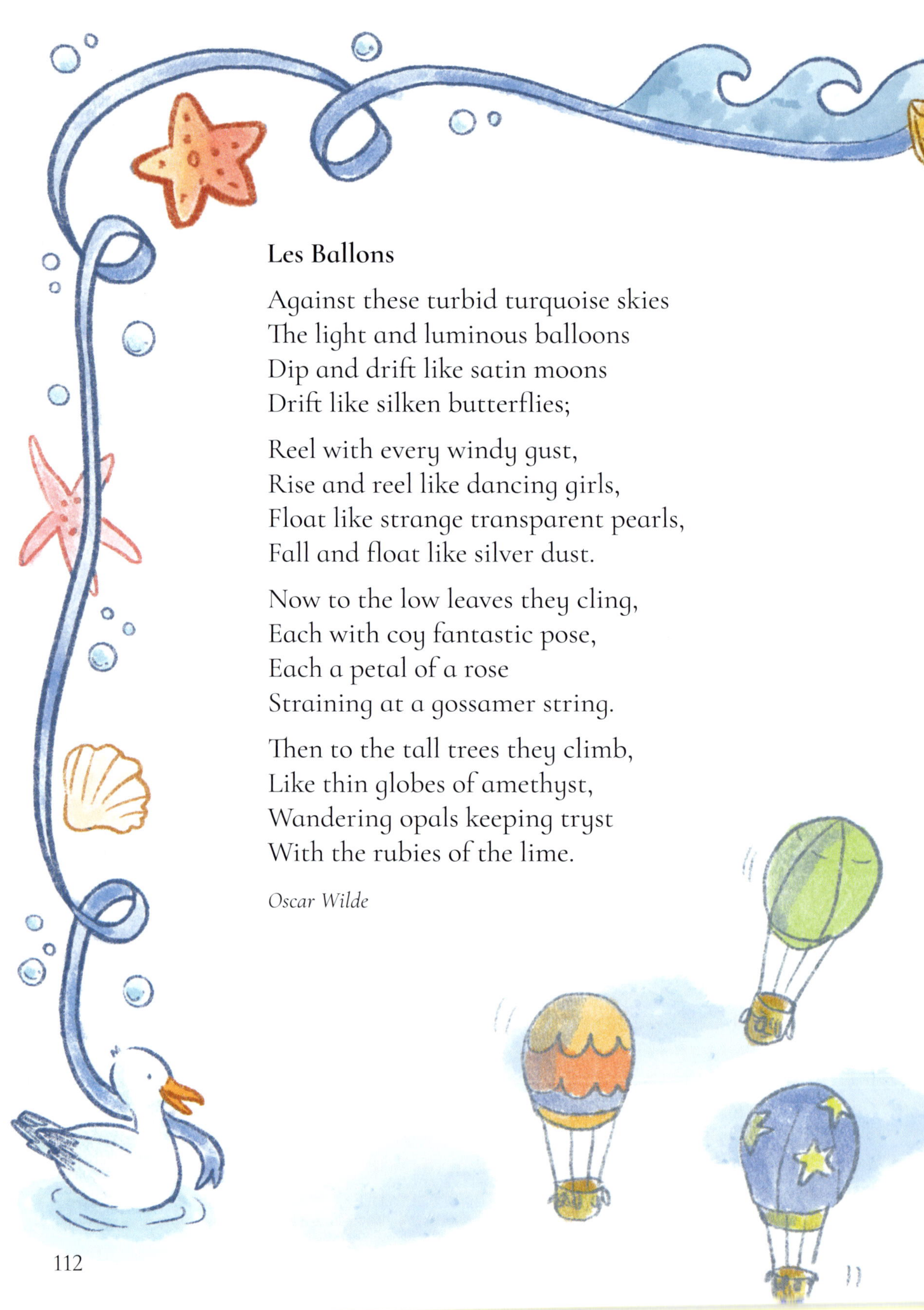

### Les Ballons

Against these turbid turquoise skies
The light and luminous balloons
Dip and drift like satin moons
Drift like silken butterflies;

Reel with every windy gust,
Rise and reel like dancing girls,
Float like strange transparent pearls,
Fall and float like silver dust.

Now to the low leaves they cling,
Each with coy fantastic pose,
Each a petal of a rose
Straining at a gossamer string.

Then to the tall trees they climb,
Like thin globes of amethyst,
Wandering opals keeping tryst
With the rubies of the lime.

*Oscar Wilde*

**St Columba's Prayer**

Be a bright flame before me, O God,
A guiding star above me.
Be a smooth path below me,
A kindly shepherd behind me
Today, tonight and for ever.
Alone with none but you, my God,
I journey on my way.
What need I fear when you are near,
O Lord of night and day.
Amen.

**Beannacht**

Go raibh míle maith agat.

## The Donkey

I saw a donkey
One day old,
His head was too big
For his neck to hold.

His legs were shaky
And long and loose,
They rocked and staggered
And weren't much use.

He tried to gambol
And frisk a bit,
But he wasn't sure
Of the trick of it.

His queer little coat
Was soft and grey,
And curled at his neck
In a lovely way.

His face was wistful,
And left no doubt
That he felt life needed
Some thinking out.

So he blundered around
In venturous quest,
And then lay flat
On the ground to rest.

He looked so little,
And weak and slim,
I prayed the world
Might be good to him.

*Anon.*

## The Butterfly

Oh, what a golden pleasure it is
To lie in the fragrant grass,
And watch the great, gaudy butterfly
As it flits and floats and glides so high,
And over the meadows pass.

Up and away, over hedge and gate,
And over the orchard wall,
It floats and it sails like a fairy boat
Where the blue sky and the white clouds float,
And the soft winds rise and fall.

*Emily Lawless*

## The Daisy

The daisy follows soft the sun,
And yellow, blue, and white
She opens wide her little door
And greets the coming light.
When the sun slips down the sky,
And soft the twilight falls,
She shuts her little door again
And creeps behind her walls.

*Emily Lawless*

## A Prayer

May God who clothes the lilies of the field,
And feeds the birds of the sky,
Who leads lambs to pasture
And guides deer to water,
Clothe us, feed us, lead us and guide us,
And change us to be more like our loving Creator.
Amen.


## The Peace Prayer of St Francis

Lord, make me an instrument of your peace:
where there is hatred, let me sow love;
where there is injury, pardon;
where there is doubt, faith;
where there is despair, hope;
where there is darkness, light;
where there is sadness, joy. Amen.

## 'June' Sang the River

'June' sang the river, 'June' sang the sky;
'June' sang the trees and the flowers together,
'June' sang the meadow-lark, 'June' sing I;
June is the month of singing weather,
June is the time for swinging clover,
Time of the old fat bee-rover,
Time for the sky to bend sweetly over,
And whisper, 'Earth dear, from the East to the West
You are lovely all seasons – but in June far the best!'

*Annette Wynne*

## Summer's Children

We are the children of summer,
Born 'neath the blossoming trees,
When the golden sun is shining,
And soft is the southern breeze.

The fields are green and the flowers are bright,
And the birds are singing gay;
We dance with delight in the warm sunlight,
For this is our own glad day.

We love the sun and the soft blue sky,
And the flowers that bloom so fair;
We laugh and we sing, and we gaily fly,
For joy is everywhere.

*Emily Lawless*

### The Table and the Chair

Said the Table to the Chair,
'You can hardly be aware
How I suffer from the heat
And from chilblains on my feet.
If we took a little walk,
We might have a little talk;
Pray let us take the air,'
Said the Table to the Chair.

Said the Chair unto the Table,
'Now, you know we are not able:
How foolishly you talk,
When you know we cannot walk!'
Said the Table with a sigh,
'It can do no harm to try.
I've as many legs as you:
Why can't we walk on two?'

So they both went slowly down,
And walked about the town
With a cheerful bumpy sound
As they toddled round and round;
And everybody cried,
As they hastened to their side,
'See! the Table and the Chair
Have come out to take the air!'

*Edward Lear*

## Blessing

The peace of God be in your heart
The grace of God be in your words
The love of God be in your hands
The joy of God be in your soul
and in the song that your life sings.


## A Butterfly Talks

A butterfly talks to each flower
And stops to eat and drink
And I have seen one lighting
In a quiet spot to think.
For there are many things he sees
That puzzle him, indeed
And I believe he thinks as well
As some who write and read.

*Annette Wynne*

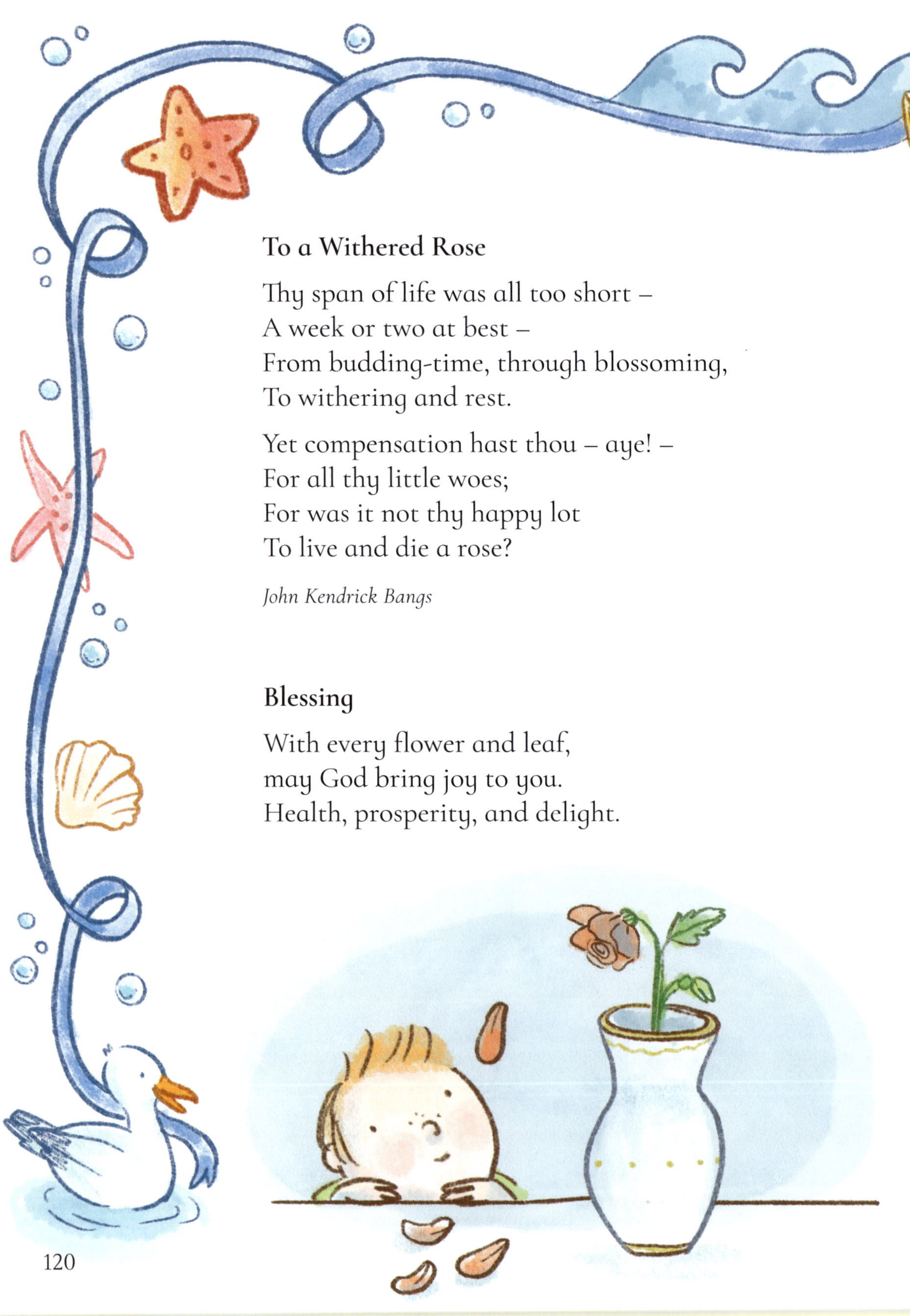

## To a Withered Rose

Thy span of life was all too short –
A week or two at best –
From budding-time, through blossoming,
To withering and rest.

Yet compensation hast thou – aye! –
For all thy little woes;
For was it not thy happy lot
To live and die a rose?

*John Kendrick Bangs*

## Blessing

With every flower and leaf,
may God bring joy to you.
Health, prosperity, and delight.

**Grace before Meals**

Our hands we fold,
Our heads we bow:
For food and drink
We thank you now.


**Blessing**

May luck be your companion,
May friends stay by your side.
May God bless you with happiness
And may love and faith abide.

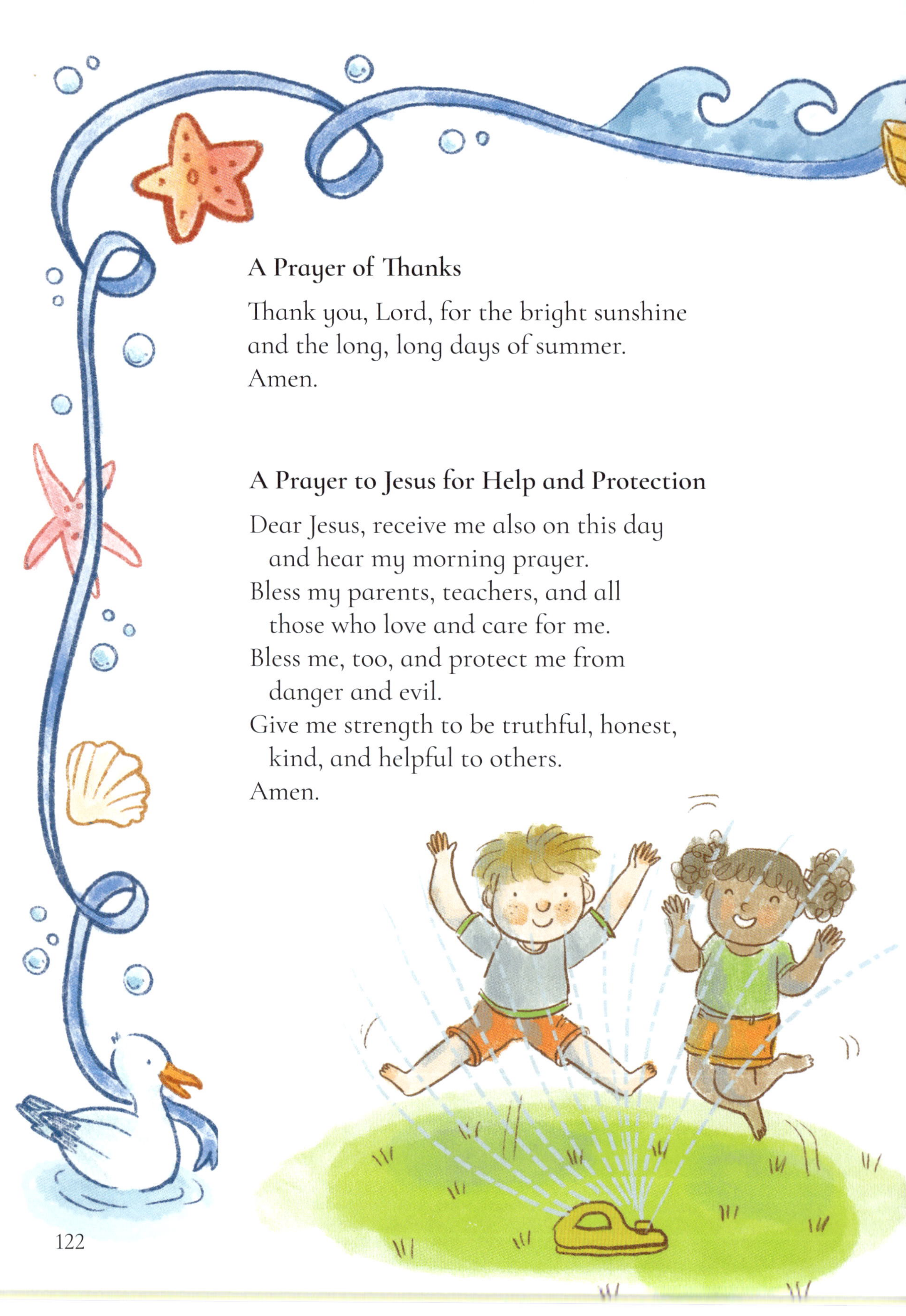

**A Prayer of Thanks**

Thank you, Lord, for the bright sunshine
and the long, long days of summer.
Amen.


**A Prayer to Jesus for Help and Protection**

Dear Jesus, receive me also on this day
    and hear my morning prayer.
Bless my parents, teachers, and all
    those who love and care for me.
Bless me, too, and protect me from
    danger and evil.
Give me strength to be truthful, honest,
    kind, and helpful to others.
Amen.

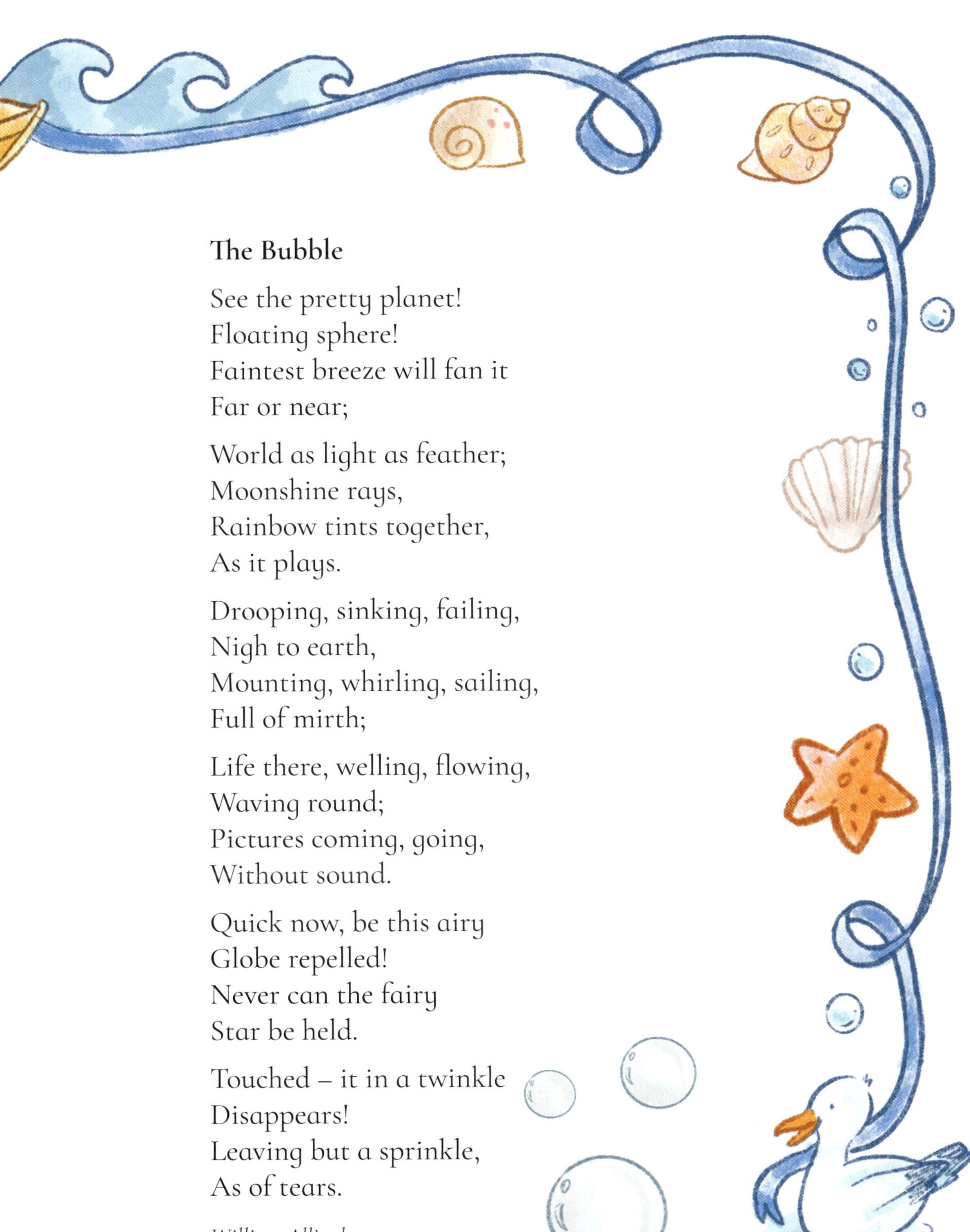

## The Bubble

See the pretty planet!
Floating sphere!
Faintest breeze will fan it
Far or near;

World as light as feather;
Moonshine rays,
Rainbow tints together,
As it plays.

Drooping, sinking, failing,
Nigh to earth,
Mounting, whirling, sailing,
Full of mirth;

Life there, welling, flowing,
Waving round;
Pictures coming, going,
Without sound.

Quick now, be this airy
Globe repelled!
Never can the fairy
Star be held.

Touched – it in a twinkle
Disappears!
Leaving but a sprinkle,
As of tears.

*William Allingham*

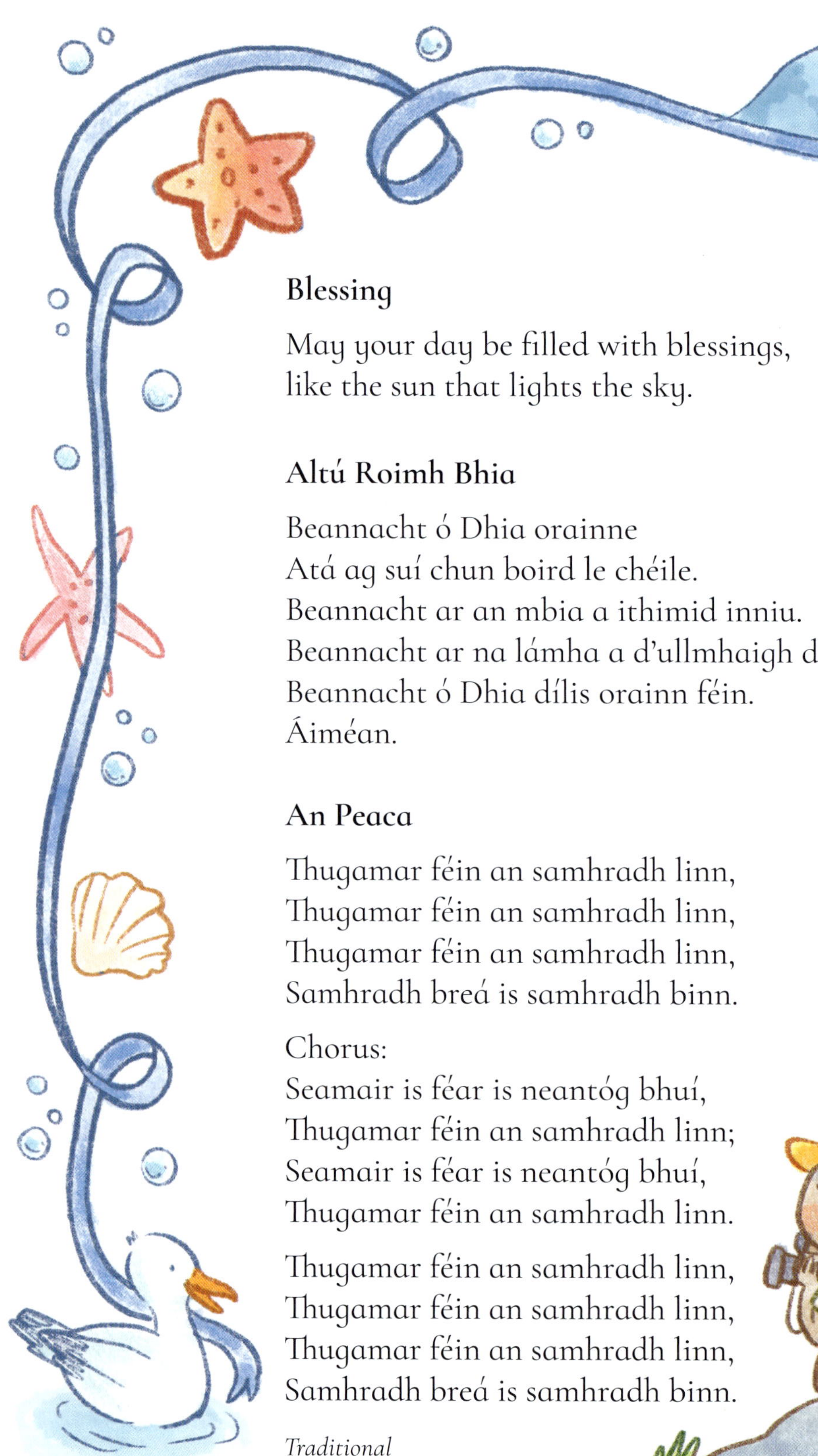

### Blessing

May your day be filled with blessings,
like the sun that lights the sky.

### Altú Roimh Bhia

Beannacht ó Dhia orainne
Atá ag suí chun boird le chéile.
Beannacht ar an mbia a ithimid inniu.
Beannacht ar na lámha a d'ullmhaigh dúinn é.
Beannacht ó Dhia dílis orainn féin.
Áiméan.

### An Peaca

Thugamar féin an samhradh linn,
Thugamar féin an samhradh linn,
Thugamar féin an samhradh linn,
Samhradh breá is samhradh binn.

Chorus:
Seamair is féar is neantóg bhuí,
Thugamar féin an samhradh linn;
Seamair is féar is neantóg bhuí,
Thugamar féin an samhradh linn.

Thugamar féin an samhradh linn,
Thugamar féin an samhradh linn,
Thugamar féin an samhradh linn,
Samhradh breá is samhradh binn.

*Traditional*

## A Wave of the Sea

I am a wave of the sea
And the foam of the wave
And the wind of the foam
And the wings of the wind.

My soul's in the salt of the sea
In the weight of the wave
In the bubbles of foam
In the ways of the wind.

My gift is the depth of the sea
The strength of the wave
The lightness of foam
The speed of the wind.

*Joseph Mary Plunkett*

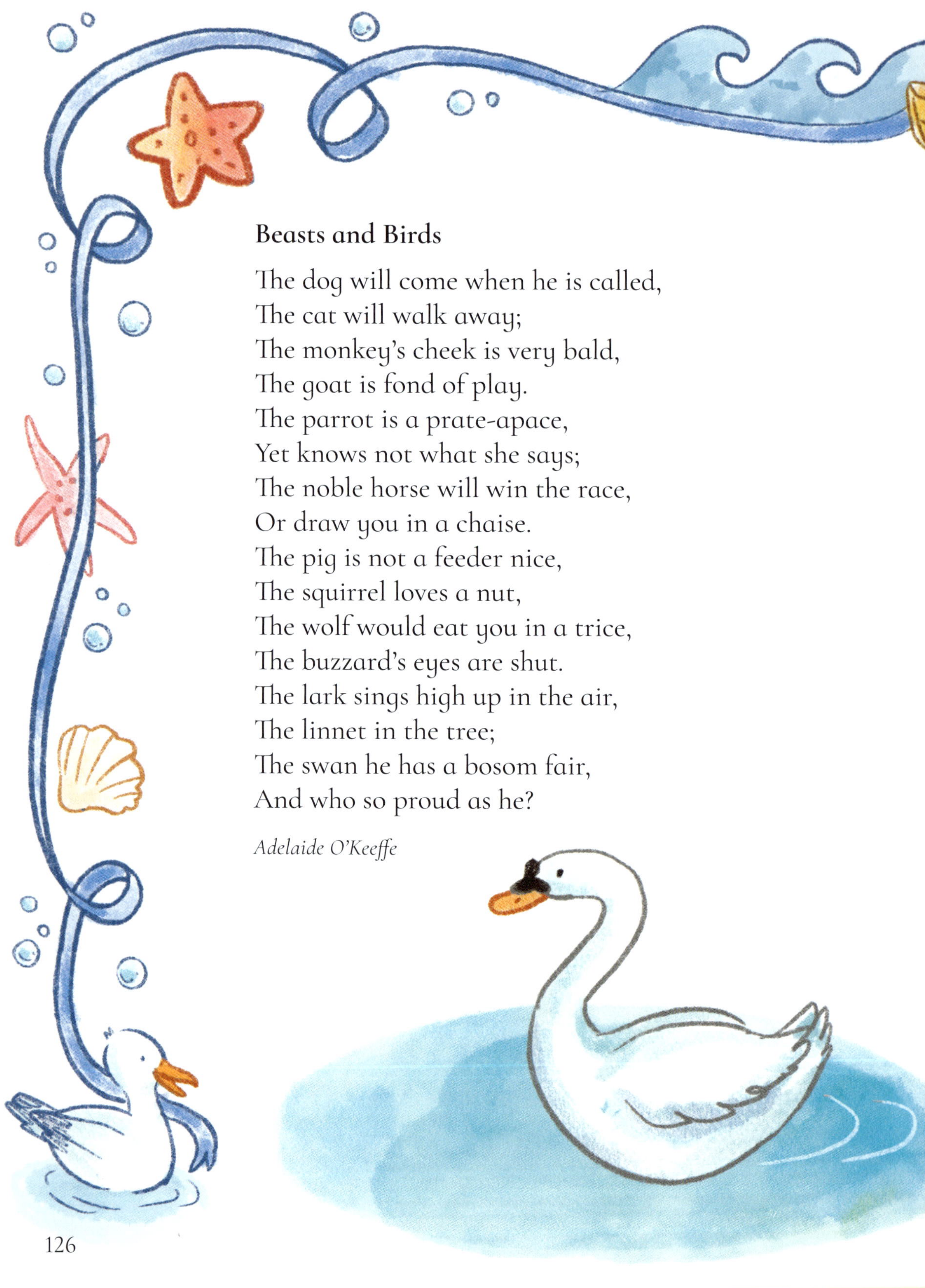

### Beasts and Birds

The dog will come when he is called,
The cat will walk away;
The monkey's cheek is very bald,
The goat is fond of play.
The parrot is a prate-apace,
Yet knows not what she says;
The noble horse will win the race,
Or draw you in a chaise.
The pig is not a feeder nice,
The squirrel loves a nut,
The wolf would eat you in a trice,
The buzzard's eyes are shut.
The lark sings high up in the air,
The linnet in the tree;
The swan he has a bosom fair,
And who so proud as he?

*Adelaide O'Keeffe*

**Blessing**

May the hinges of our friendship
never grow rusty.


**Samhradh**

Samhradh, Samhradh, is maith liom thú
An ghrian ag taitneamh, lá sa zú
Uachtar reoite, líomanáid
Ag súgradh le buicéad agus spád
Samhradh, Samhradh, is maith liom thú
Ag léim, ag rith, ag snámh
'woohoo'
Culaith shnámha, bríste gearr
Samhradh, Samhradh, an séasúr is fearr.

*Sinéad McNally*

# JULY

It's official! Summer is here, the holidays have begun and the heat is rising. In July we can enjoy the simple pleasures of playing and eating outdoors. The days seem endless, with the sun rising early in the morning and setting late in the evening.

**Prayer for the Summer**

Dear God,
Thank you for giving us this wonderful time
together with our friends and family. Thank you
for the sun and the sea, and picnics on the beach.
Thank you for the clear skies at night, when we can
see the stars spread across the heavens. Amen.

# Iúil

**Bed in Summer**

In winter I get up at night
And dress by yellow candle-light.
In summer, quite the other way,
I have to go to bed by day.
I have to go to bed and see
The birds still hopping on the tree,
Or hear the grown-up people's feet
Still going past me in the street.
And does it not seem hard to you,
When all the sky is clear and blue,
And I should like so much to play,
To have to go to bed by day?

*Robert Louis Stevenson*

### The Shadow People

Old Lame Brigid doesn't hear
Fairy music in the grass
When the gloaming's on the mere
And the shadow people pass:
Never hears their tiny feet
Coming from the village street
Just beyond the parson's wall,
Where the clover globes are sweet
And the mushroom's parasol
Opens in the moonlit rain.

Every night I hear them call
From their long and merry train.
Old Lame Brigid says to me
'It is just your fancy, child.'

She cannot believe I see
Laughing faces in the wild,
Hands that twinkle in the sedge
Bowing at the water's edge
Where the finny minnows quiver,
Shaping on a blue wave's ledge
Bubble foam to sail the river.
And the sunny hands to me
Beckon ever, beckon ever.
Oh! I would be wild and free
And with the shadow people be.

*Francis Ledwidge*

## The Canticle of Brother Sun

Be praised, my Lord, through all your creatures,
especially through my lord Brother Sun,
who brings the day; and you give light through him.
And he is beautiful and radiant in all his splendour!
Of you, Most High, he bears the likeness.

Be praised, my Lord, through Sister Moon and the stars;
in the heavens you have made them bright,
precious and beautiful.

*St Francis of Assisi*


## Beannacht

Go lonraí an ghrian go te ar d'aghaidh,
go dtite an bháisteach go mín ar do pháirceanna,
agus go dtí go mbuailimid le chéile arís,
go gcoinní Dia tú i mbos a láimhe thú.

## The Song of Wandering Aengus

I went out to the hazel wood,
Because a fire was in my head,
And cut and peeled a hazel wand,
And hooked a berry to a thread;
And when white moths were on the wing,
And moth-like stars were flickering out,
I dropped the berry in a stream
And caught a little silver trout.

When I had laid it on the floor
I went to blow the fire aflame,
But something rustled on the floor,
And someone called me by my name:
It had become a glimmering girl
With apple blossom in her hair
Who called me by my name and ran
And faded through the brightening air.

Though I am old with wandering
Through hollow lands and hilly lands,
I will find out where she has gone,
And kiss her lips and take her hands;
And walk among long dappled grass,
And pluck till time and times are done
The silver apples of the moon,
The golden apples of the sun.

*W.B. Yeats*

## A Prayer

As the sun rises, Lord, let your light shine on me.
Amen.


## Paidir na Maidine

A Dhia, tá grá agat dom.
Bíonn tú liom de lá is d'oíche.
Ba mhaith liom grá a thabhairt duit
Gach nóiméad den lá.
Ba mhaith liom tú a shásamh.
A Athair, cabhraigh liom.
Áiméan.

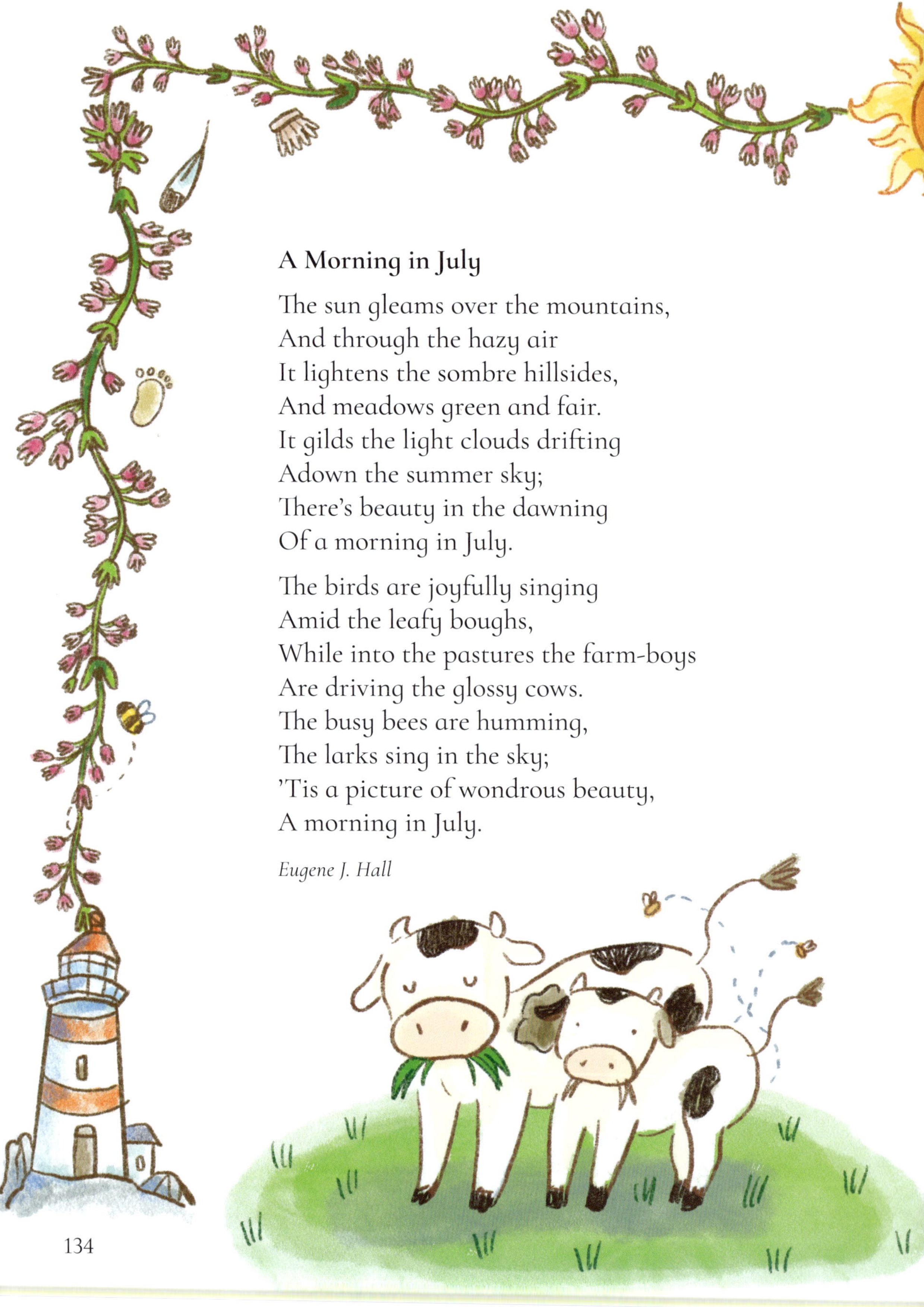

## A Morning in July

The sun gleams over the mountains,
And through the hazy air
It lightens the sombre hillsides,
And meadows green and fair.
It gilds the light clouds drifting
Adown the summer sky;
There's beauty in the dawning
Of a morning in July.

The birds are joyfully singing
Amid the leafy boughs,
While into the pastures the farm-boys
Are driving the glossy cows.
The busy bees are humming,
The larks sing in the sky;
'Tis a picture of wondrous beauty,
A morning in July.

*Eugene J. Hall*

### Eitleog

Scaoilim m'eitleog
Suas suas san aer.
Pógann sí na crainn,
Is preabann chun na spéire.
Éalaíonn isteach i scamall,
Is tosaíonn sí ag spraoi,
Ag luascadh is ag eitilt
Le rithim na gaoithe.

Ba bhreá liomsa bheith i m'eitleog
Thuas in airde sa spéir.
Ba bhreá liom dul ar foluain
Ar sciatháin aeir.
Ba bhreá liom bheith léi
Thuas os cionn na gcrann ag spraoi,
Ag lorg faoisimh
Ón uaigneas seo i mo chroí.

*Áine Ní Ghlinn*

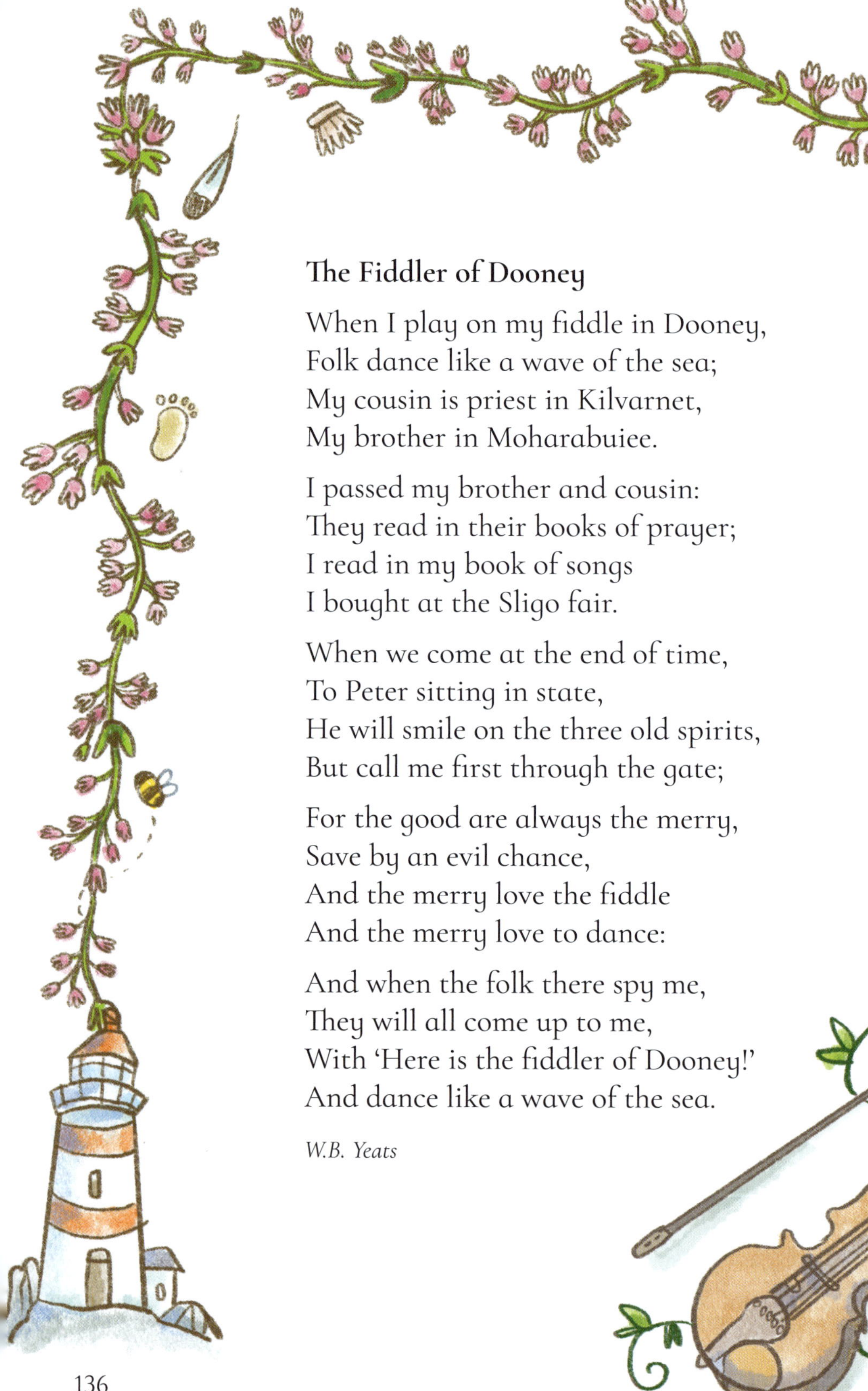

## The Fiddler of Dooney

When I play on my fiddle in Dooney,
Folk dance like a wave of the sea;
My cousin is priest in Kilvarnet,
My brother in Moharabuiee.

I passed my brother and cousin:
They read in their books of prayer;
I read in my book of songs
I bought at the Sligo fair.

When we come at the end of time,
To Peter sitting in state,
He will smile on the three old spirits,
But call me first through the gate;

For the good are always the merry,
Save by an evil chance,
And the merry love the fiddle
And the merry love to dance:

And when the folk there spy me,
They will all come up to me,
With 'Here is the fiddler of Dooney!'
And dance like a wave of the sea.

*W.B. Yeats*

### An Evening Prayer

Dear Jesus,
Thank you for this day,
Thank you for my family and the good
friends we got to see today,
Help us have a good night's rest and a
happy day tomorrow,
In Jesus' name, we pray, Amen.

### Grace before Meals

Our hands we fold,
Our heads we bow:
For food and drink
We thank you now.
Amen.

### A Prayer of Thanks

For football and tennis: we thank you, O Lord.
For swimming and running: we thank you, O Lord.
For lying and thinking: we thank you, O Lord.
For talking and dreaming: we thank you, O Lord.
For all that makes summer so lovely: we thank you,
O Lord. Amen.

### Blessing

May you live and prosper under the bright
King of the world.

## The Happy Little Clock

In my garret room, I'm never quite alone.
I have a small companion all my own,
A cunning, round-faced merry little elf,
My little china clock upon the shelf.
It's tick, tick, ticking all the day,
How I love its cheery steady little way.
It keeps my garret room
Free from sprites of fear and gloom,
The happy little clock upon the shelf.

It calls me every morning to my work,
In rain or shine it never tries to shirk;
The cozy little, honest little elf,
The busy little clock upon the shelf;
O it's tick, tick ticking day and night,
It ticks its 'honest best' with all its might;
I shall never lack a friend
When my daytime labours end
With my little china clock upon the shelf.

*Annette Wynne*

## A Prayer of Thanks

All the good gifts around us
Are sent from heaven above.
We thank the Lord for his love. Amen.


## An Evening Prayer

Dear Lord,
When the sun is setting
And the sky changes colour very, very slowly
And very beautifully,
We thank you for the wonder of our world. Amen.

## The Wind that Shakes the Barley

There's music in my heart all day,
I hear it late and early,
It comes from fields are far away,
The wind that shakes the barley.

Above the uplands drenched with dew
The sky hangs soft and pearly,
An emerald world is listening to
The wind that shakes the barley.

Above the bluest mountain crest
The lark is singing rarely,
It rocks the singer into rest,
The wind that shakes the barley.

Oh, still through summers and through springs
It calls me late and early.
Come home, come home, come home, it sings,
The wind that shakes the barley.

*Katharine Tynan*

## A Prayer of Thanks

Dear Lord,
Thank you for the long, long days of summer.
Thank you for the sandy beaches and the
sweet-smelling grass under our bare feet. Amen.

## Dawn

Quiet miles of golden sky,
And in my heart a sudden flower.
I want to clap my hands and cry
For Beauty in her secret bower.

Quiet golden miles of dawn –
Smiling all the East along;
And in my heart nigh fully blown,
A little rose-bud of a song.

*Francis Ledwidge*

## A Prayer

Dear Lord,
The young sparrows are being fed,
Their wings are beating,
They open their mouths very wide ...
Lord of the sparrows,
Help us to realise how much you love
    each one of us
Just because we are. Amen.

## Blessing

Bless the house wherein you live,
Bless every window, wall and door.
Bless everyone beneath its roof
And every hand that works to keep
    all safe within.

## Summer Sun

Great is the sun, and wide he goes
Through empty heaven without repose;
And in the blue and glowing days
More thick than rain he showers his rays.

Though closer still the blinds we pull
To keep the shady parlour cool,
Yet he will find a chink or two
To slip his golden fingers through.

Meantime his golden face around
He bares to all the garden ground,
And sheds a warm and glittering look
Among the ivy's inmost nook.

Above the hills, along the blue,
Round the bright air with footing true,
To please the child, to paint the rose,
The gardener of the World, he goes.

*Robert Louis Stevenson*

## A Prayer

Dear Lord, in these long, warm days life slows
down and we have time for picnics and days at
the beach or pool.

Help me to rest in the cool shade of your love.
Fill my heart with kindness towards everyone I
meet this summer. Amen.

## The Moon

The moon shone bright and the stars gave light,
And away to the forest I sped;
But the day had come with its bright, warm sun,
And the fairies were all fled.

*Anon.*

### The Painting

Under the rose-tree's dancing shade
There stands a little ivory girl,
Pulling the leaves of pink and pearl
With pale green nails of polished jade.

The red leaves fall upon the mould,
The white leaves flutter, one by one,
Down to a blue bowl where the sun,
Like a great dragon, writhes in gold.

The white leaves float upon the air,
The red leaves flutter idly down,
Some fall upon her yellow gown,
And some upon her raven hair.

She takes an amber lute and sings,
And as she sings a silver crane
Begins his scarlet neck to strain,
And flap his burnished metal wings.

With pale green nails of polished jade,
Pulling the leaves of pink and pearl,
There stands a little ivory girl
Under the rose-tree's dancing shade.

*Oscar Wilde*

## Blessing

May God give you,
for every storm, a rainbow,
for every tear, a smile,
for every care, a promise
and blessing in each trial.
For every problem life sends,
a faithful friend to share,
for every sign a sweet song,
and an answer for each prayer.

## The Little Waves of Breffny

The grand road from the mountain goes
   shining to the sea,
And there is traffic in it, and many a horse
   and cart;
But the little roads of Cloonagh are dearer
   far to me,
And the little roads of Cloonagh go
   rambling through my heart.

*Eva Gore-Booth (extract)*

# August

August is the harvest month, when all the crops planted in spring are gathered and stored. It's also the time for sunny holidays or long days out at the seaside, swimming and playing in the water with our families and friends.

We thank God for all his gifts – the crops in the ground waiting to be gathered, the sun on our faces when we meet our friends outdoors, our families who love and provide for us. We give thanks for all the good things in our lives.

**A Summer Prayer**

Dear God,
This summer will be
full of new experiences
for me and my friends:
exciting new games
and holidays to places
we've never been before.
Grow us, stretch us
through whatever we do,
and through wherever we go,
so that we'll end the summer
just a little more like you. Amen.

 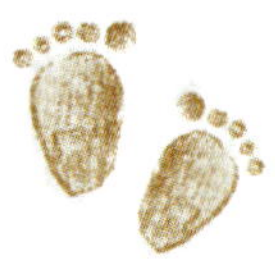

# Lúnasa

**Chorus of Spirits**

Gently! – gently! – down! – down!
From the starry courts on high,
Gently step adown, down
The ladder of the sky.
Sunbeam steps are strong enough
For such airy feet:
Spirits, blow your trumpets rough,
So as they be sweet!
Breathe them loud, the Queen descending,
Yet a lowly welcome breathe,
Like so many flowerets bending
Zephyr's breezy foot beneath.

*George Darley*

## Symphony in Yellow

An omnibus across the bridge
Crawls like a yellow butterfly
And, here and there, a passer-by
Shows like a little restless midge.

Big barges full of yellow hay
Are moored against the shadowy wharf,
And, like a yellow silken scarf,
The thick fog hangs along the quay.

The yellow leaves begin to fade
And flutter from the Temple elms,
And at my feet the pale green Thames
Lies like a rod of rippled jade.

*Oscar Wilde*

## Beannacht

Beannacht Dé ar an obair.

## A Summer Blessing

May you walk with God
This summer
In whatever you do
And wherever you go.

## In the Poppy Field

Mad Patsy said, he said to me,
That every morning he could see
An angel walking on the sky;
Across the sunny skies of morn
he threw great handfuls far and nigh
Of poppy seed among the corn;
And then, he said, the angels run
To see the poppies in the sun.

*James Stephens*

## Gairdín Mhamó

Na bláthanna áille
Na crainn sean is óga
Ag fás i rith na bliana
I ngairdín Mhamó

Oibríonn sí go dian
Amuigh faoin spéir
Aimsir go deas is go dona
Na míonna go léir

Is áit suaimhneach is spreagúil
É gairdín Mhamó
Is tugann sé faoiseamh
Le sórt fuinneamh beo

*Sinéad McNally*

## A Prayer of Thanks

For salty sea and sunny skies,
For walks on mountains and hillsides,
For time to rest and time to play,
Thank you, God, for holidays. Amen.

## Blessing

I see the moon,
The moon sees me,
God bless all my friends.
And God bless me.

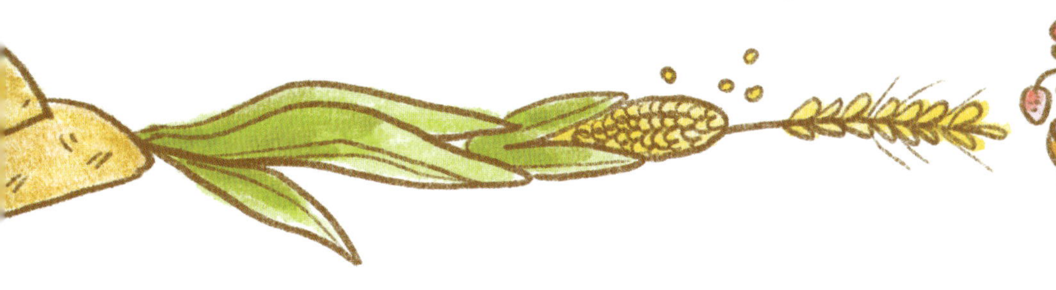

## The Rushes

The rushes nod by the river
As the winds on the loud waves go,
And the things they nod of are many,
For it's many the secret they know.

And I think they are wise as the fairies
Who lived ere the hills were high,
They nod so grave by the river
To everyone passing by.

*Francis Ledwidge*

## The Balloon

I climbed a cloud
and there I found a moon,
With sleepy and shining
face beneath the sun.

*James Stephens*

**A Morning Prayer**

Dear Lord, please help me to be good today and
to do what is right.
Help me to listen well and to be kind to others.
Amen.

**A Aingeal Uasail**

A Aingeal Uasail,
A Aingeal Dé,
Cuidigh liom ar feadh an lae.
Bí le m'ais go síoraí dlúth,
Agus ná lig domsa dul amú.
Áiméan.

## Twinkle, Twinkle, Little Star

Twinkle, twinkle, little star,
How I wonder what you are!
Up above the world so high,
Like a diamond in the sky.

When the blazing sun is gone,
When he nothing shines upon,
Then you show your little light,
Twinkle, twinkle, all the night.

Then the traveller in the dark
Thanks you for your tiny spark,
How could he see where to go,
If you did not twinkle so?

In the dark blue sky you keep,
Often through my curtains peep
For you never shut your eye,
Till the sun is in the sky.

As your bright and tiny spark
Lights the traveller in the dark,
Though I know not what you are,
Twinkle, twinkle, little star.

*Jane Taylor*

### A Prayer of Thanks

Thank you, Lord, for this world
Your creation
Rolled into a sphere
Packaged in sunshine
Gift-wrapped in love
And given to us.
Amen.

### Blessing

God greet you, all gathered here,
May God and Mary greet you.

## A Child's Evensong

The sun is weary, for he ran
So far and fast today;
The birds are weary, for who sang
So many songs as they?
The bees and butterflies at last
Are tired out; for just think, too,
How many gardens through the day
Their little wings have fluttered through.

And so, as all tired people do,
They've gone to lay their sleepy heads
Deep, deep in warm and happy beds.
The sun has shut his golden eye,
And gone to sleep beneath the sky;
The birds, and butterflies, and bees
Have all crept into flowers and trees,
And all lie quiet, still as mice.

*Richard Le Gallienne*

## August Heat

In August, when the days are hot,
I like to find a shady spot,
And hardly move a single bit –
And sit –
And sit –
And sit –
And sit!

*Anon.*

## The Wind

The wind is a jolly fellow,
He comes from the west and east,
He whistles and sings in the tree-tops,
And dines with the birds at feast.
He dances along the meadows,
And skips o'er the waves at sea,
And the flowers bow down to greet him,
For a rollicking rogue is he.

*Emily Lawless*

## The Irish Wolfhound

As fly the shadows o'er the grass,
He flies with step as light and sure,
He hunts the wolf through Tostan pass,
And starts the deer by Lisanoure.
The music of the Sabbath bells,
O Con! has not a sweeter sound
Than when along the valley swells
The cry of John Mac Donnell's hound.
His stature tall, his body long,
His back like night, his breast like snow,
His foreleg pillar-like and strong,
His hindleg like a bended bow;
Rough curling hair, head long and thin,
His ear a leaf so small and round;
Not Bran, the favourite dog of Fin,
Could rival John Mac Donnell's hound.

*Denis Florence MacCarthy*

## A Morning Prayer

Lord, let your love and your
  joy shine upon us
And make our hearts glad.
Amen.

### The Boy Who Never Told a Lie

Once there was a little boy,
With curly hair and pleasant eye –
A boy who always told the truth,
And never, never told a lie.

And when he trotted off to school,
The children all about would cry,
'There goes the curly-headed boy –
The boy that never tells a lie.'

And everybody loved him so,
Because he always told the truth,
That every day, as he grew up,
'Twas said, 'There goes the honest youth.'

And when the people that stood near
Would turn to ask the reason why,
The answer would be always this:
'Because he never tells a lie.'

*Anon.*

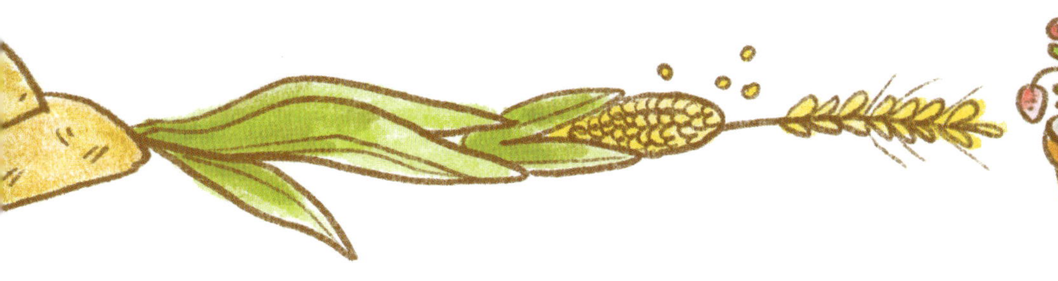

## Blessing

May the grace of God's protection and his
great love abide within your home and within
the hearts of all who live inside.

## The Magic Dress

I saw a child upon the street
Who wore a dress of flowered silk,
And, oh, it was a lovely thing,
For my delight did bubble up.

*James Stephens*

## A Prayer

Dear Lord,
The sun is golden in a pure blue sky,
The grass in the meadows ripples softly in the breeze,
A sky-lark pierces the air with his sweet song,
And in the hedgerows butterflies bask in the warmth.
And everything,
Everything,
Seems to be singing its own song of praise
To you, our Lord and our God.
Amen.

## The Last Rose of Summer

'Tis the last rose of Summer,
Left blooming alone;
All her lovely companions
Are faded and gone;
No flower of her kindred,
No rose-bud is nigh,
To reflect back her blushes
Or give sigh for sigh!

*Thomas Moore (extract)*

### A Prayer of Thanks

For the softness of moss
We thank you, O Lord.
For the strength of the oak tree,
We thank you, O Lord.
For the fragrance of roses,
We thank you, O Lord.
For all the plants in the world
We thank you, O Lord.
Amen.

### Weather

Whether the weather be fine
Or whether the weather be not,
Whether the weather be cold
Or whether the weather be hot,
We'll weather the weather
Whatever the weather,
Whether we like it or not.

*Anon.*

## A Morning Prayer

Dear Lord, may we accept this day
As a gift to be treasured,
A life to be enjoyed,
A trust to be kept,
And a hope to be fulfilled;
And all for your glory.
Amen.

## The Happy Apple

If I were an apple and grew on a tree,
I think I'd fall down on a nice boy like me;
I wouldn't stay there giving nobody joy,
I'd fall down at once and say: 'Eat me, my boy.'

*Anon.*

## Blessing

God bless all my friends
God bless my brothers and sisters
God bless everyone.

### An Gabhar sa Scoil

Isteach sa scoil shiúil seanghabhar
Is shuigh síos ar stól;
Thóg sé fód as lár na tine
Is d'ith sé é mar lón.

As a phóca thóg sé leabhairín grinn,
Is thosaigh sé ag léamh;
Rinne sé rince dúinn ansin,
'S a mheigheall thuas san aer.

D'ól sé dúch as buidéal,
Is thaitin leis, ar ndóigh.
Chuir sé píopa cré 'na bhéal,
Is chaith sé é go beo.

Ag dul amach an doras dó
Chaoch sé súil amháin;
'Is iontach an áit an scoil' ar sé,
'Ach b'fhearr liom bheith i bpáirc'.

*Seán Mac Fheorais*

### A Prayer of Thanks

Dear Lord, thank you for this bright new
day. Help me to make it a good one for
everyone I meet today.
Amen.

### Blessing

If happiness were a dessert so sweet
May life give you more than you can ever eat.

### A Prayer

Lord, let your love and your joy
   shine upon us
And make our hearts glad – this
   lovely day and for ever.
Amen.

**August Night**

We had to wait for the heat to pass,
And I was lying on the grass,

While Mother sat outside the door,
And I saw how many stars there were.

Beyond the tree, beyond the air,
And more and more were always there.

So many that I think they must
Be sprinkled on the sky like dust.

A dust is coming through the sky!
And I felt myself begin to cry.

So many of them and so small,
Suppose I cannot know them all.

*Elizabeth Madox Roberts*

 # SEPTEMBER 

Although it has one foot in summer and one in autumn, September marks the beginning of a new season in nature – the harvest is in and it's the time for planting winter crops. The leaves are already changing colour, though autumn officially begins at the equinox towards the end of the month.

Many schools start back in September, which often makes it feel as if it is the beginning of a new year. We ask God to help us with the challenges of moving up in school, or going to a new school, especially if none of our friends are with us.

# MEÁN FÓMHAIR

## Two Little Shadows

I saw a young mother
With eyes full of laughter
And two little shadows
Came following after.
Wherever she moved,
They were always right there
Holding onto her skirts,
Hanging onto her chair.
Before her, behind her –
An adhesive pair.
'Don't you ever get weary

As, day after day,
your two little tagalongs
Get in your way?'
She smiled as she shook
Her pretty young head,
And I'll always remember
The words that she said.
'It's good to have shadows
That run when you run,
That laugh when you're happy
And hum when you hum –
For you only have shadows
When your life's filled with sun.'

*Anon.*

### Walk to School

Before the land of doors and bells, dusty books and
luncheon smells he walks a walk of calm and breeze,
Magpie birds and maple trees.
There's one for sorrow and two for joy,
Why is it four for a boy?

He kicks through the leaves about to turn red
Now they are fallen crunching and dead.
The birch leaves fall like summer rain,
When will they grow again?

He sees a fox of fire and white,
Only caught before in the dead of night.
Where does he live? In a hole?
So many questions before school ...

*Joe Potter*

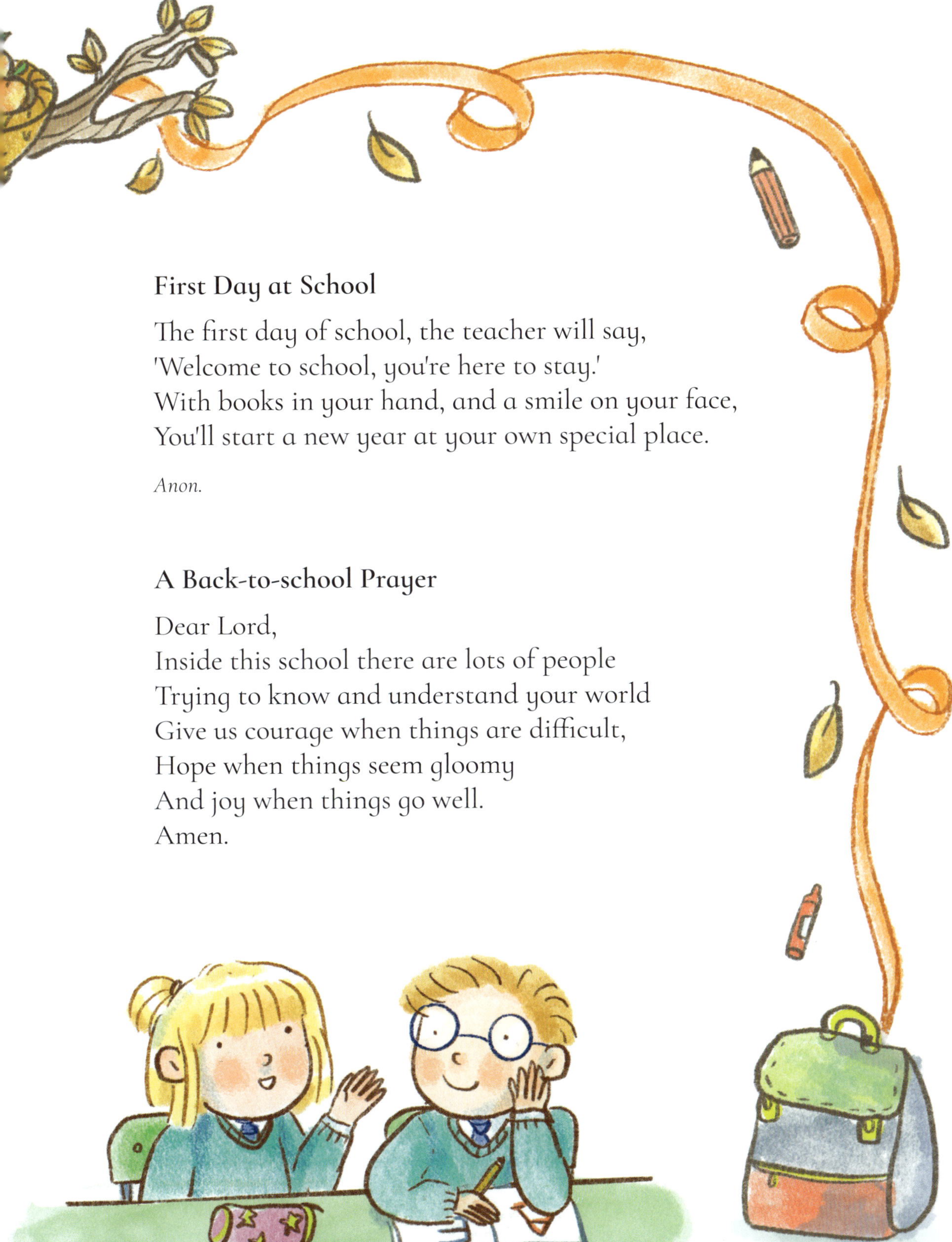

**First Day at School**

The first day of school, the teacher will say,
'Welcome to school, you're here to stay.'
With books in your hand, and a smile on your face,
You'll start a new year at your own special place.

*Anon.*


**A Back-to-school Prayer**

Dear Lord,
Inside this school there are lots of people
Trying to know and understand your world
Give us courage when things are difficult,
Hope when things seem gloomy
And joy when things go well.
Amen.

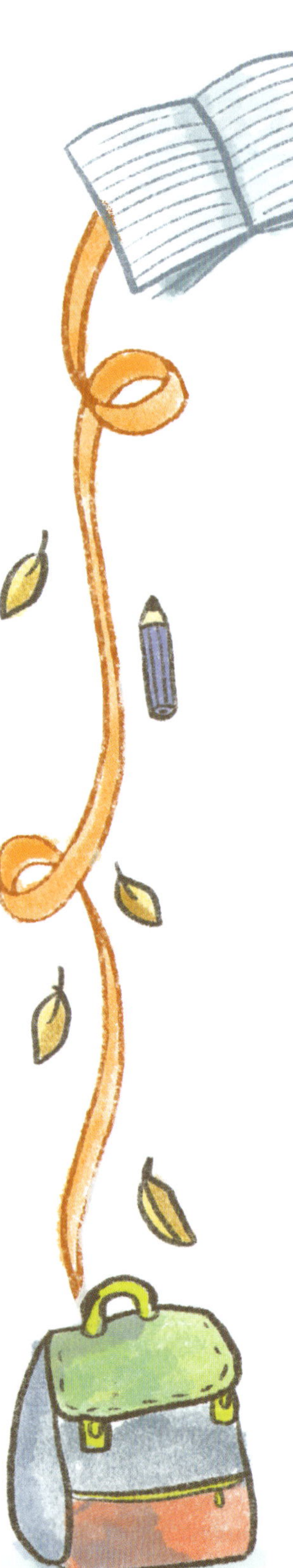

## A Prayer

Lord,
May we accept this day,
As a gift to be treasured,
A life to be enjoyed,
A trust to be kept,
And a hope to be fulfilled;
And all for your glory.
Amen.

## Among School Children

I walk through the long schoolroom questioning;
A kind old nun in a white hood replies;
The children learn to cipher and to sing,
To study reading-books and history,
To cut and sew, be neat in everything
In the best modern way – the children's eyes
In momentary wonder stare upon
A sixty-year-old smiling public man.

*W.B. Yeats*

## Grace before Meals

The grace of God and the favour of Patrick
On all that I see and that I do.
The blessing that God put on the five loaves
And two fish, may he put on this food too.
Amen.


## An Grá

Le cuileog bhacach
Bhuail damhán alla tráth
Is dá n-ainneoin féin,
Thit an bheirt i ngrá.
Pósadh iad ag cóisir mhór,
Is ar mhí na meala d'imigh siad leo.

An lá dar gcionn, go mór faoi léan,
D'fhill an damhán alla is é leis féin.
'Ar mo chomhaireamh atá an locht –
Bhí mé cinnte go bhfuair mé a hocht;
Dallta ag an ngrá a bhí me, muise,
Níor thug mé faoi deara na maidí croise.

*Éamonn Ó Ruanaí*

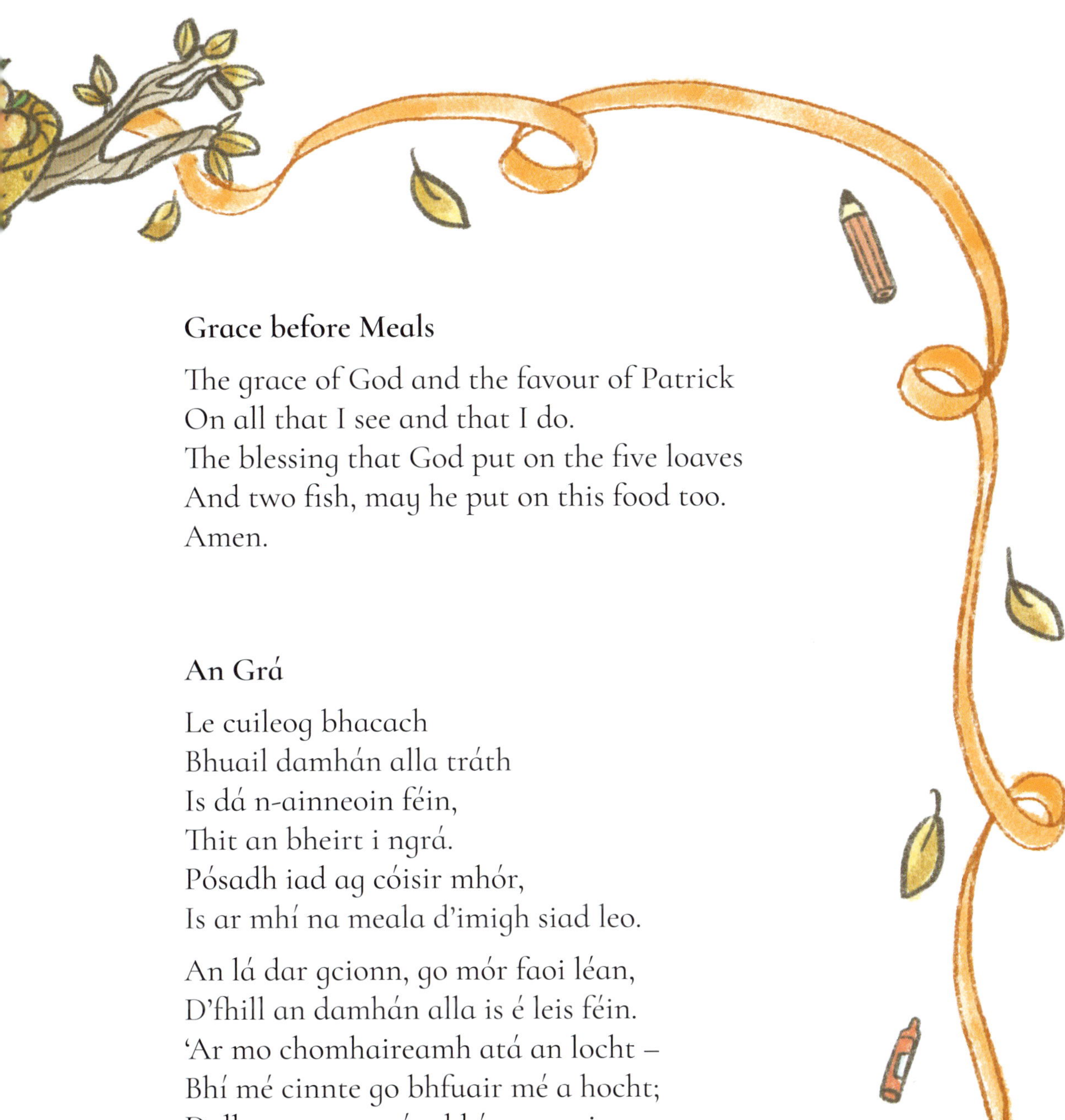

## The Swing

How do you like to go up in a swing,
Up in the air so blue?
Oh, I do think it the pleasantest thing
Ever a child can do!

Up in the air and over the wall,
Till I can see so wide,
Rivers and trees and cattle and all
Over the countryside –

Till I look down on the garden green,
Down on the roof so brown –
Up in the air I go flying again,
Up in the air and down!

*Robert Louis Stevenson*

## A Morning Prayer

This morning the mist is softly gliding
Around the lamp-posts and trees.
Everything looks different ...
Thank you, God, for the unexpected jewels
of your world.
Amen.

## A Prayer at Bedtime

Angels bless
And angels keep;
Angels guard me
While I sleep.
Amen.

## Paidir na hOíche

A Dhia, a Athair, molaim thú
As ucht do chineáltais liom inniu.
As ucht mo chairde molaim thú,
Agus as an teaghlach a thug tú dom.
I ndorchadas na hoíche cosain mé
Solas na maidine go bhfeice mé.
Áiméan.

## What Robin Told

How do robins build their nests?
Robin Redbreast told me –
First a wisp of yellow hay
In a pretty round they lay;
Then some shreds of downy floss,
Feathers, too, and bits of moss,
Woven with a sweet, sweet song,
This way, that way, and across;
That's what Robin told me.

Where do robins hide their nests?
Robin Redbreast told me –
Up among the leaves so deep,
Where the sunbeams rarely creep,
Long before the winds are cold,
Long before the leaves are gold,
Bright-eyed stars will peep and see
Baby robins – one, two, three;
That's what Robin told me.

*George Cooper*

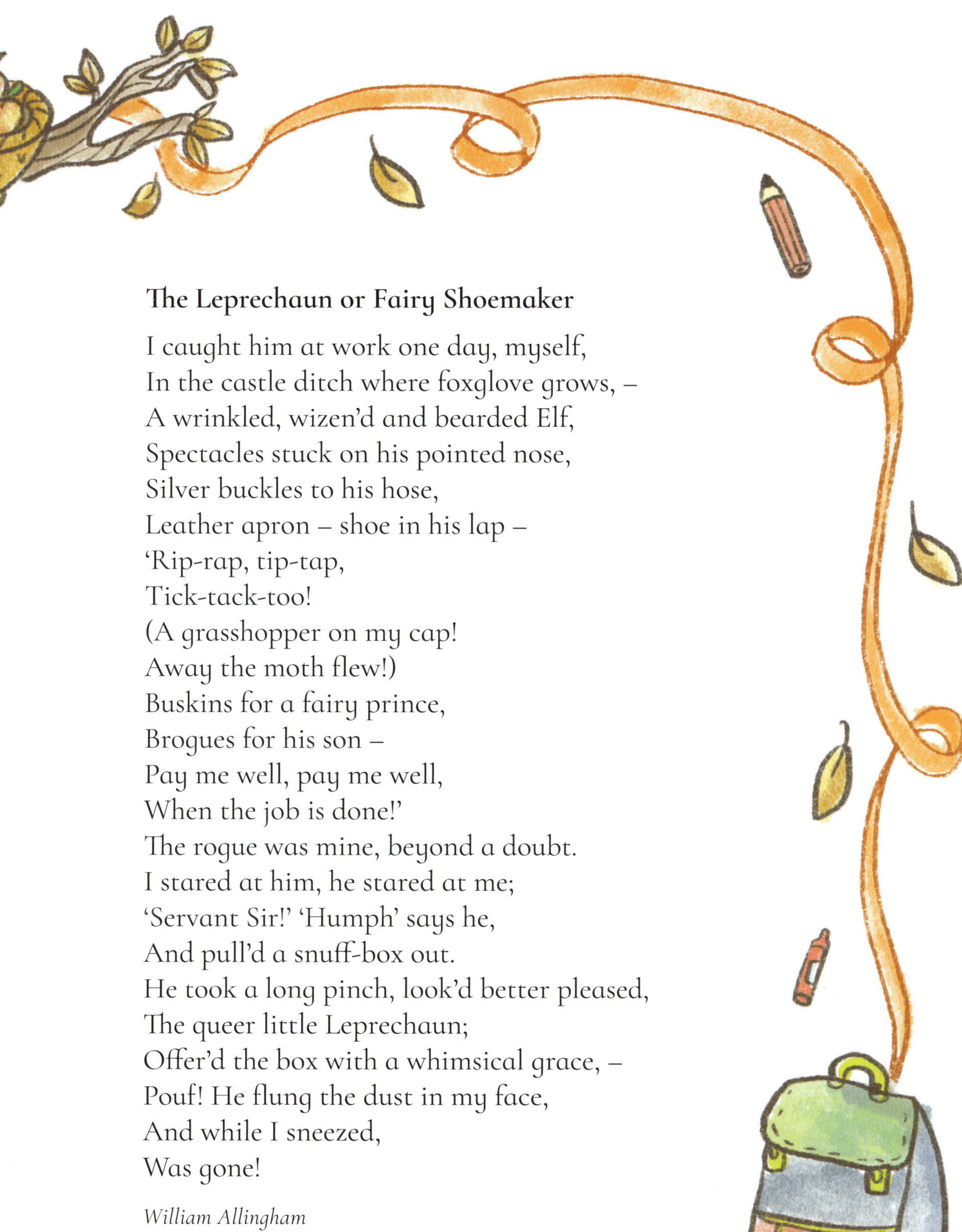

## The Leprechaun or Fairy Shoemaker

I caught him at work one day, myself,
In the castle ditch where foxglove grows, –
A wrinkled, wizen'd and bearded Elf,
Spectacles stuck on his pointed nose,
Silver buckles to his hose,
Leather apron – shoe in his lap –
'Rip-rap, tip-tap,
Tick-tack-too!
(A grasshopper on my cap!
Away the moth flew!)
Buskins for a fairy prince,
Brogues for his son –
Pay me well, pay me well,
When the job is done!'
The rogue was mine, beyond a doubt.
I stared at him, he stared at me;
'Servant Sir!' 'Humph' says he,
And pull'd a snuff-box out.
He took a long pinch, look'd better pleased,
The queer little Leprechaun;
Offer'd the box with a whimsical grace, –
Pouf! He flung the dust in my face,
And while I sneezed,
Was gone!

*William Allingham*

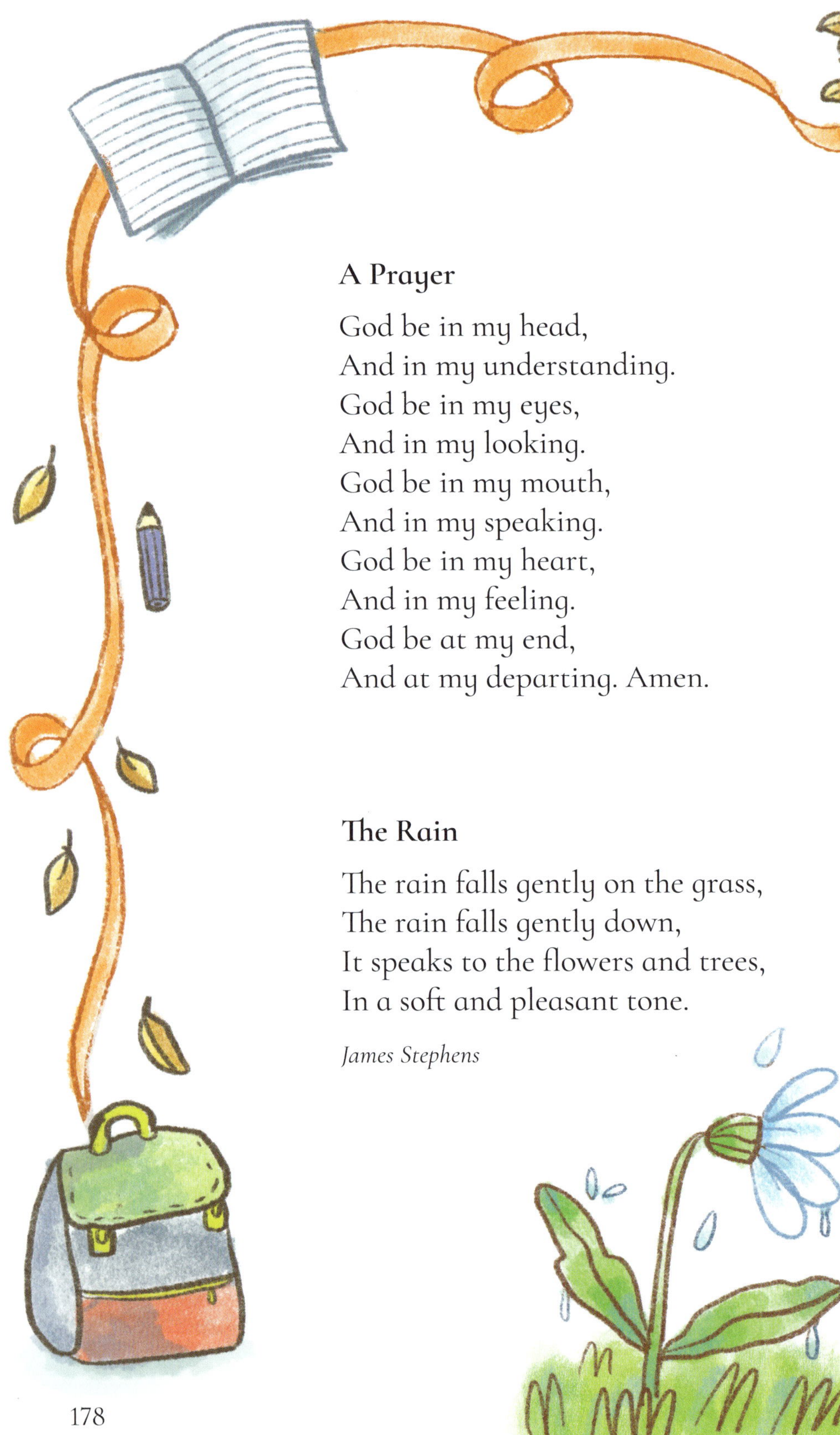

## A Prayer

God be in my head,
And in my understanding.
God be in my eyes,
And in my looking.
God be in my mouth,
And in my speaking.
God be in my heart,
And in my feeling.
God be at my end,
And at my departing. Amen.

## The Rain

The rain falls gently on the grass,
The rain falls gently down,
It speaks to the flowers and trees,
In a soft and pleasant tone.

*James Stephens*

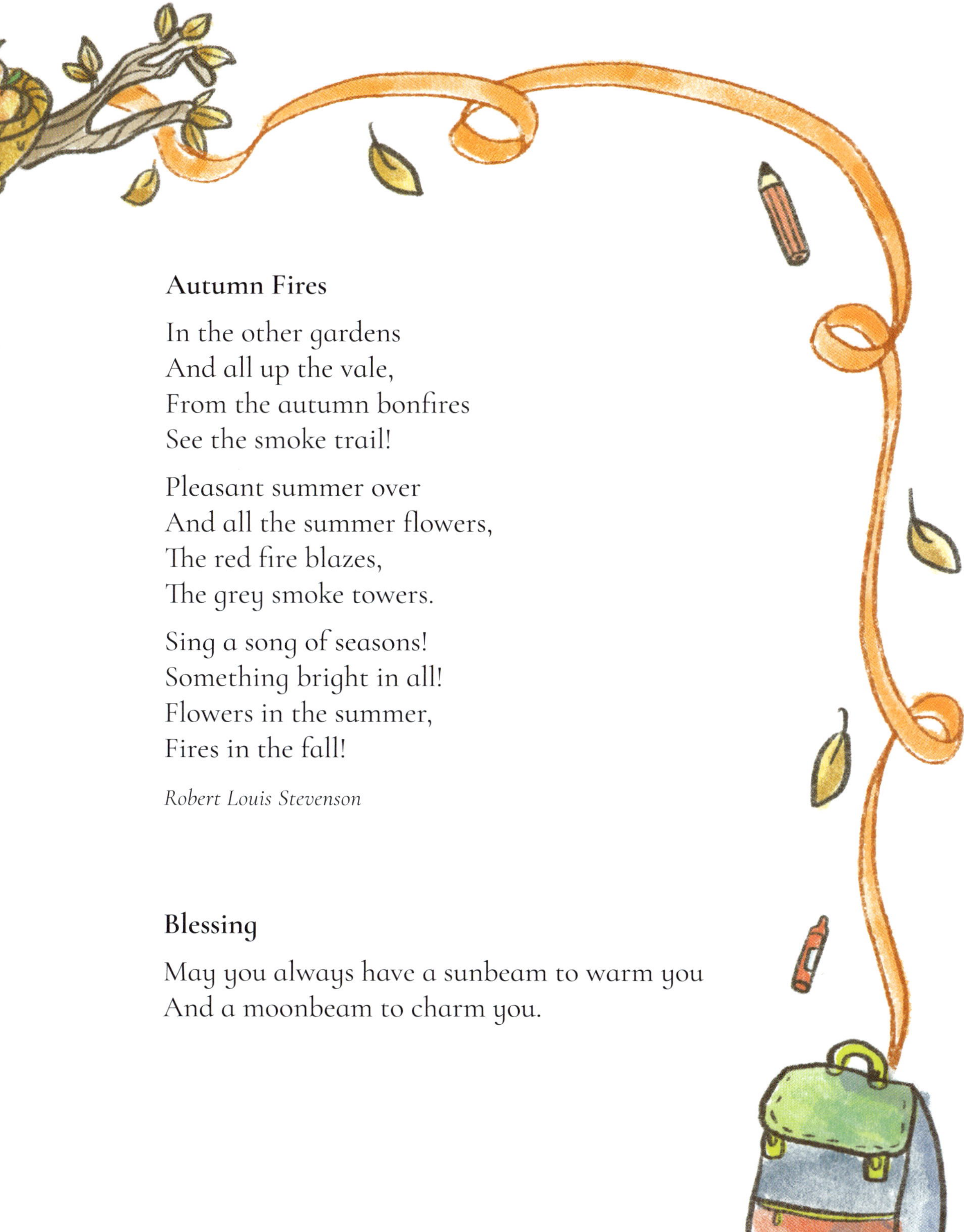

## Autumn Fires

In the other gardens
And all up the vale,
From the autumn bonfires
See the smoke trail!

Pleasant summer over
And all the summer flowers,
The red fire blazes,
The grey smoke towers.

Sing a song of seasons!
Something bright in all!
Flowers in the summer,
Fires in the fall!

*Robert Louis Stevenson*

## Blessing

May you always have a sunbeam to warm you
And a moonbeam to charm you.

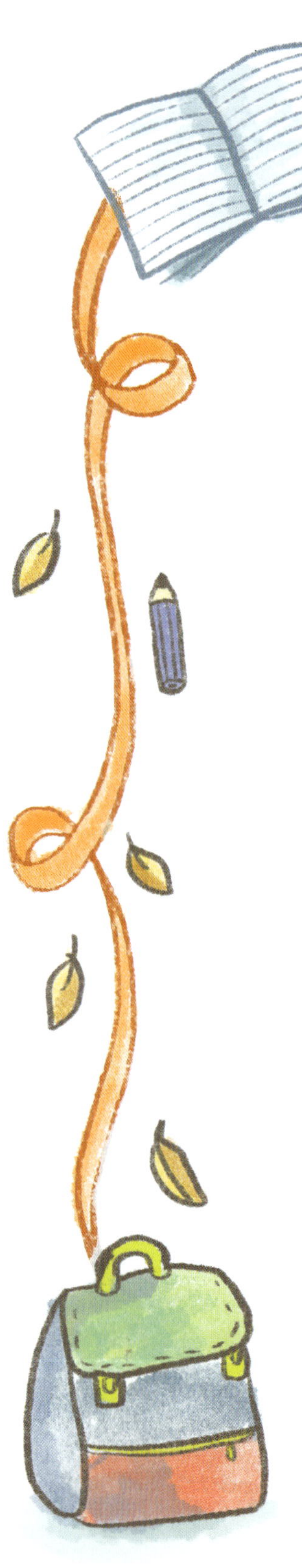

## Good Morning, Jesus

Jesus, you are good and wise
I will praise you when I rise.
Jesus, hear this prayer I send
Bless my family and my friends.
Jesus, help my eyes to see
All the good you send to me.
Amen.

## Beannacht

Go gcastar an t-ádh leat.

## The Road to Fairyland

O, I know a road that leads to a land
Where the fairies dance their hours away,
They dance and they play with the flowerets gay,
And they hide in the forest shade.

*Dora Sigerson Shorter*

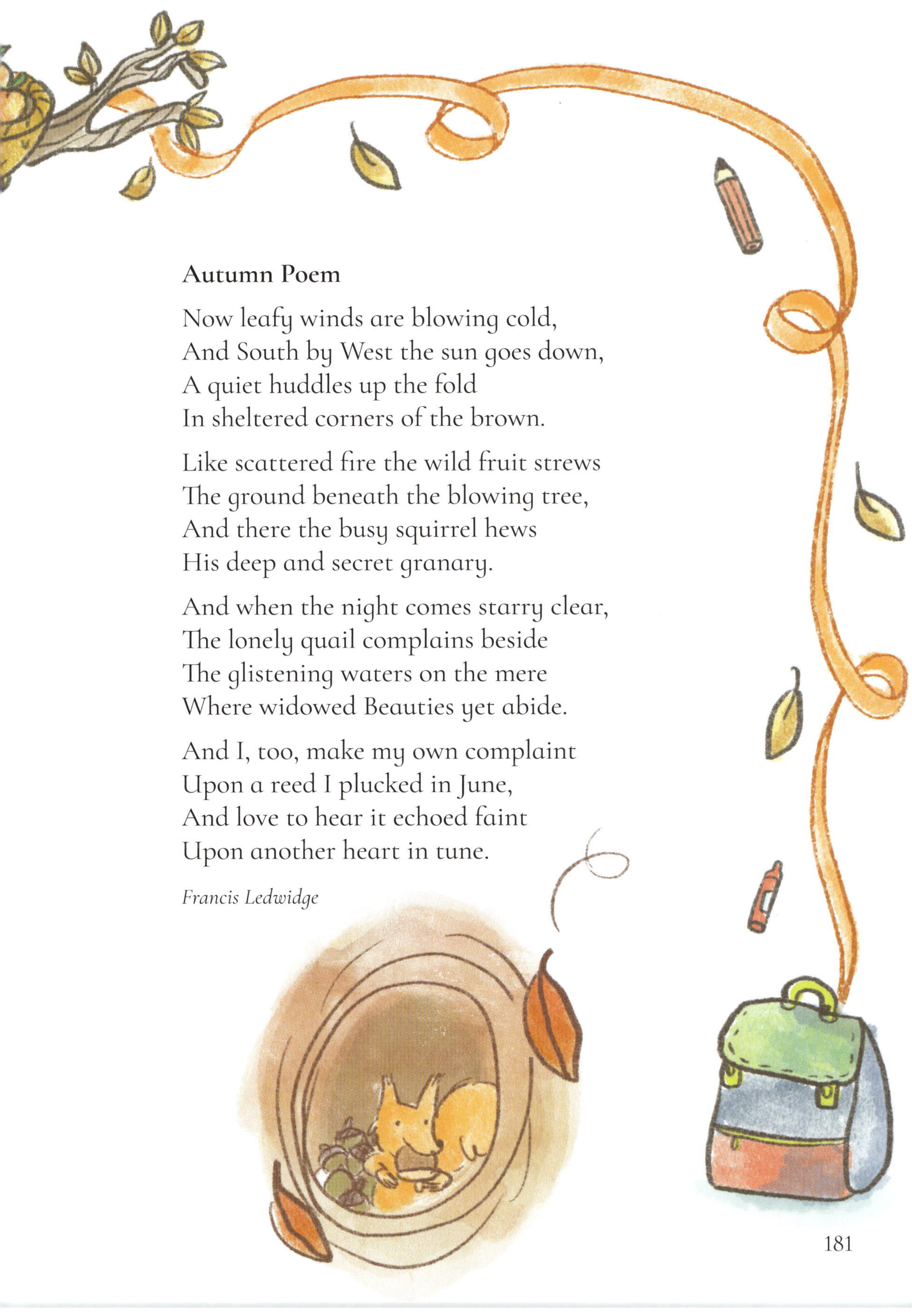

## Autumn Poem

Now leafy winds are blowing cold,
And South by West the sun goes down,
A quiet huddles up the fold
In sheltered corners of the brown.

Like scattered fire the wild fruit strews
The ground beneath the blowing tree,
And there the busy squirrel hews
His deep and secret granary.

And when the night comes starry clear,
The lonely quail complains beside
The glistening waters on the mere
Where widowed Beauties yet abide.

And I, too, make my own complaint
Upon a reed I plucked in June,
And love to hear it echoed faint
Upon another heart in tune.

*Francis Ledwidge*

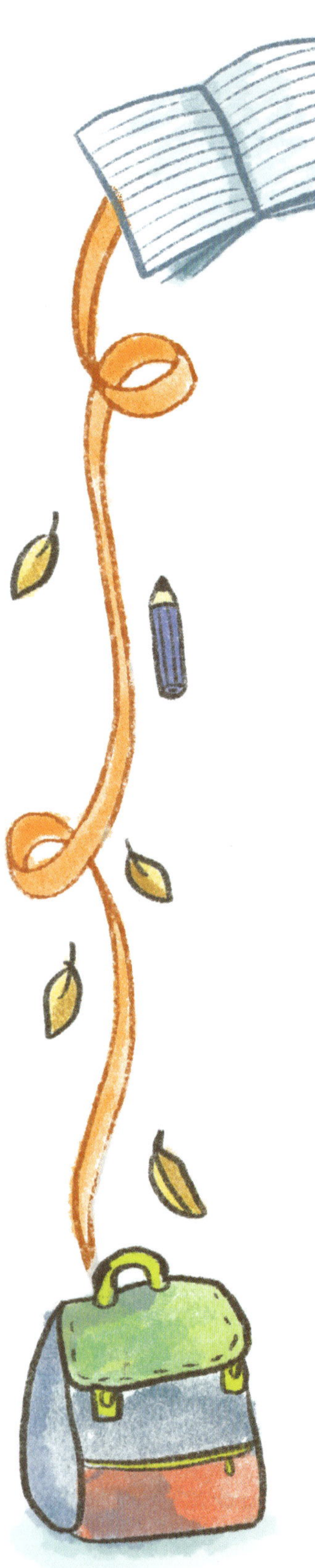

### A Prayer of Thanks

Dear Lord, your generous love surrounds us,
And everything we enjoy comes from you.
Thank you for all your gifts to us.
Amen.


### Blessing

May there always be work for your hands to do;
May your purse always hold a coin or two;
May the sun always shine on your windowpane;
May a rainbow be certain to follow each rain;
May the hand of a friend always be near you;
May God fill your heart with gladness to cheer you.

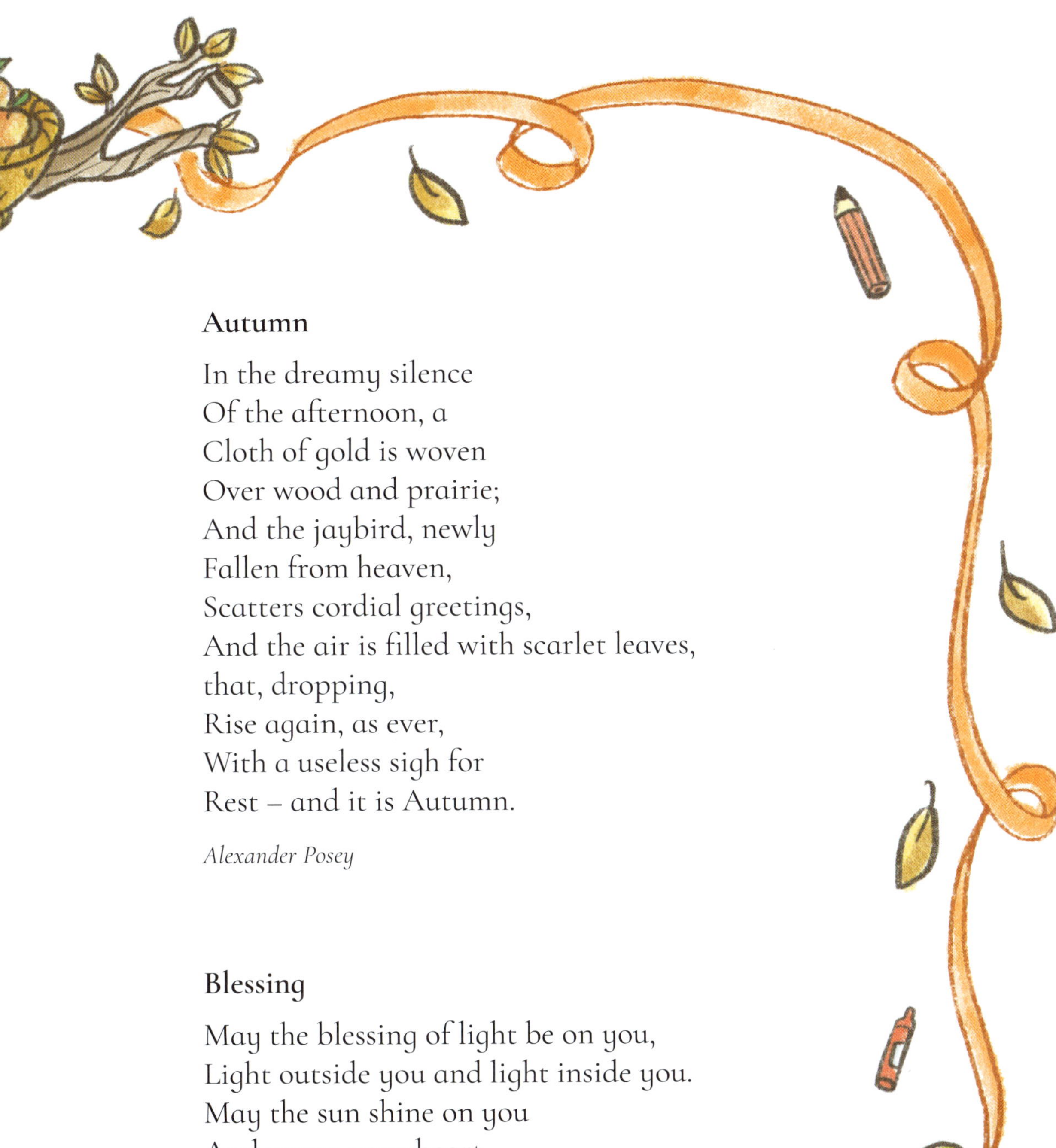

## Autumn

In the dreamy silence
Of the afternoon, a
Cloth of gold is woven
Over wood and prairie;
And the jaybird, newly
Fallen from heaven,
Scatters cordial greetings,
And the air is filled with scarlet leaves,
that, dropping,
Rise again, as ever,
With a useless sigh for
Rest – and it is Autumn.

*Alexander Posey*

## Blessing

May the blessing of light be on you,
Light outside you and light inside you.
May the sun shine on you
And warm your heart
Till it glows like a great turf fire.

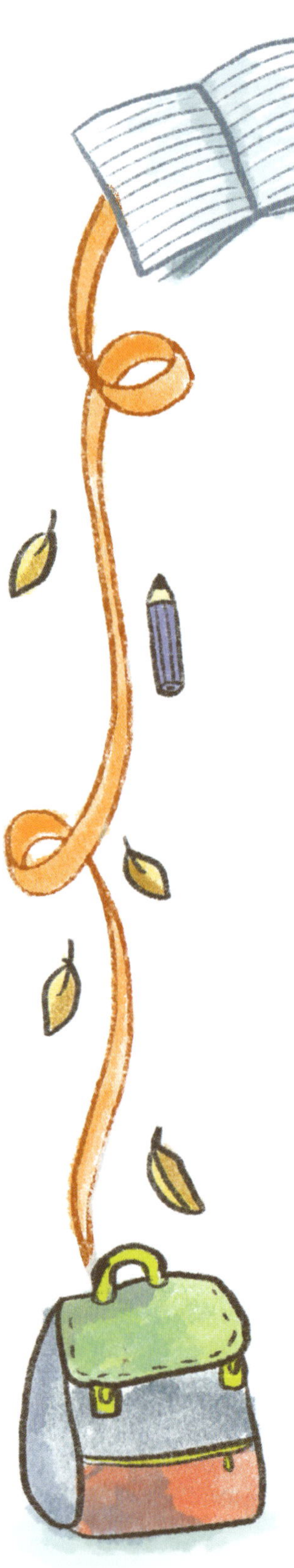

### A Prayer

God in heaven, hear my prayer,
keep me in your loving care.
Be my guide in all I do,
Bless all those who love me too.
Amen.

### In Autumn

They're coming down in showers,
The leaves all gold and red;
They're covering the little flowers,
And tucking them in bed
They've spread a fairy carpet
All up and down the street;
And when we skip along to school,
They rustle neath our feet.

*Winifred C. Marshall*

### A Blessing Prayer

God bless all those I love;
God bless all those who love me;
God bless all those that love those I love
And all those that love those who love me.
Amen.

### A Prayer of Thanks

Thank you, Jesus,
for all my friends at school
and for my teachers
who teach me new things every day. Amen.

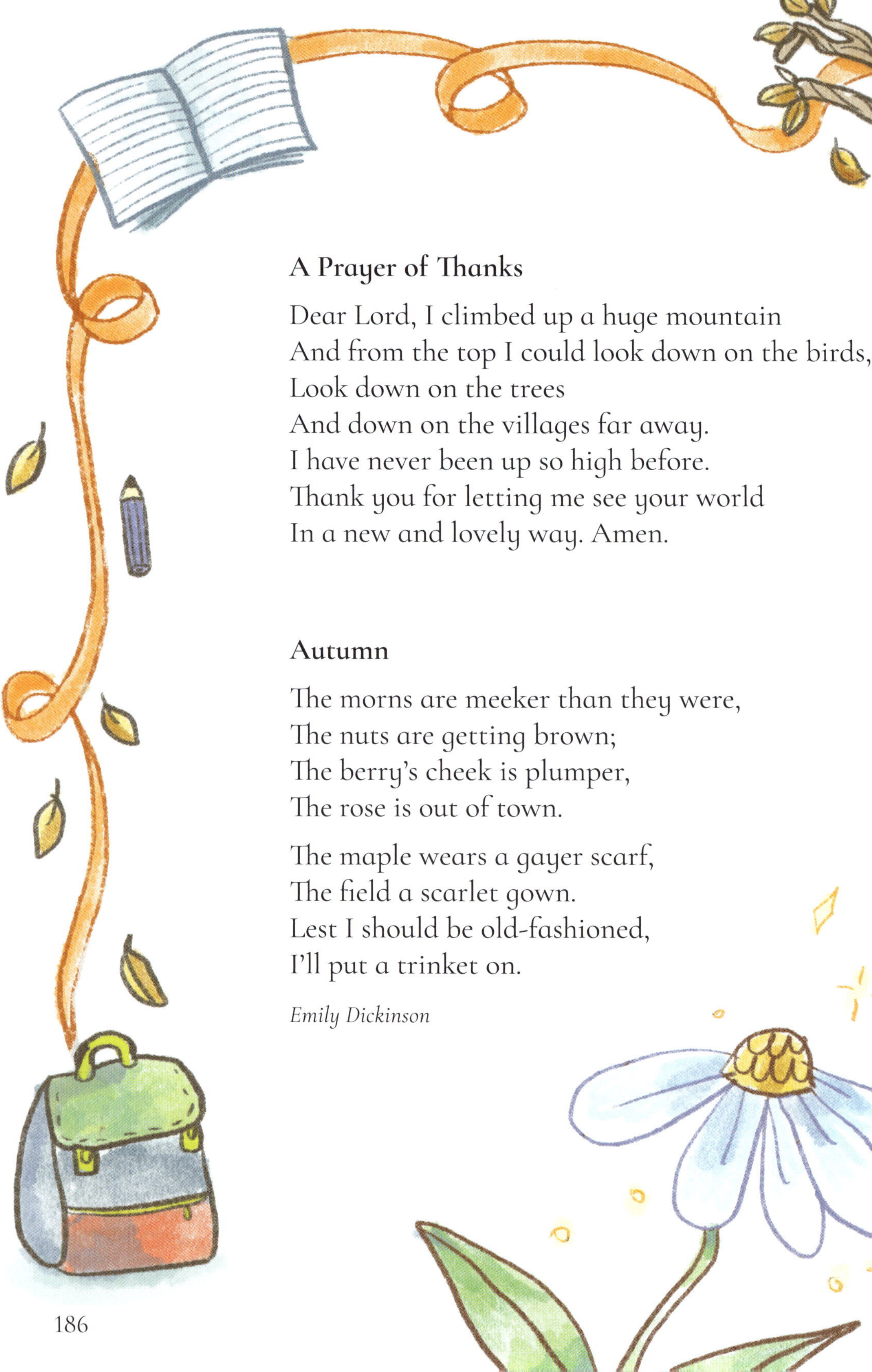

## A Prayer of Thanks

Dear Lord, I climbed up a huge mountain
And from the top I could look down on the birds,
Look down on the trees
And down on the villages far away.
I have never been up so high before.
Thank you for letting me see your world
In a new and lovely way. Amen.


## Autumn

The morns are meeker than they were,
The nuts are getting brown;
The berry's cheek is plumper,
The rose is out of town.

The maple wears a gayer scarf,
The field a scarlet gown.
Lest I should be old-fashioned,
I'll put a trinket on.

*Emily Dickinson*

**Merry Autumn Days**

'Tis pleasant on a fine spring morn
To see the buds expand.
'Tis pleasant in the summertime
To see the fruitful land;
'Tis pleasant on a winter's night
To sit around the blaze,
But what joys like these, my boys,
To merry autumn days!

*Charles Dickens*


**Thank You, Lord**

Leaves sigh,
Whisper,
Glide,
And flop to the ground.
Thank you Lord, for the surprising
And quiet sounds of the world.

# OCTOBER

We are now getting deep into autumn – the days are shorter, the air is cool and crisp, and the glorious blaze of autumn colours is all around us. Soon the leaves will carpet the ground, apples will appear in the kitchen and we will have to think ahead to winter, and what it might bring.

The carefree days of summer are over, but we thank God for all the good things that autumn brings into our lives.

**An Autumn Prayer**

We praise you, God, for golden leaves.
We praise you, God, for gentle mists.
We praise you, God, for apples and fruit.
We praise you, God, for chestnuts and conkers.
We praise you, God, for a glorious world. Amen.

# Deireadh Fómhair

**Leaves**

I love to see the leaves go by
In Autumn's sunny air;
They flutter and they fall, and lie
On earth with colors rare.

They dance upon the breezes light
And twirl in graceful play;
They sparkle in the sunshine bright,
And then are swept away.

Yet while they fall, they seem to say
To children young and old,
That life is but a summer day
With many tales to be told.

*Marjorie Pickthall*

## A Prayer

We cannot see the wind blowing;
We can only see the trees bending in its path;
We can only see the ripples stirring the surface
Of the water.
We cannot see your Spirit, Lord,
But only the movement in people's lives
Caused by your love.
Amen.

## Aedh Wishes for the Cloths of Heaven

Had I the heavens' embroidered cloths,
Enwrought with golden and silver light,
The blue and the dim and the dark cloths
Of night and light and the half-light,
I would spread the cloths under your feet:
But I, being poor, have only my dreams;
I have spread my dreams under your feet;
Tread softly because you tread on my dreams.

*W.B. Yeats*

## Fall, Leaves, Fall

Fall, leaves, fall; die, flowers, away;
Lengthen night and shorten day;
Every leaf speaks bliss to me
Fluttering from the autumn tree.

I shall smile when wreaths of snow
Blossom where the rose should grow;
I shall sing when night's decay
Ushers in a drearier day.

*Emily Brontë*


## Beannacht

Fad ar do shaol agus laethanta geala.

### A Prayer of Thanks

Dear Jesus, thank you for all the lovely autumn colours which we can enjoy as our world gets ready to put on its winter coat.
Amen.

### Paidir don Spiorad Naomh

Spiorad Dé sna spéartha.
Spiorad Dé sna farraigí.
Spiorad Dé ar na sléibhte.
Spiorad Dé ionam.
Spiorad Dé i solas na gréine.
Spiorad Dé san aer.
Spiorad Dé thart timpeall orainn.
Spiorad Dé i ngach áit.
A Spioraid Naoimh, Spiorad Dé,
  cabhraigh Liom.
Áiméan.

## October's Party

October gave a party;
The leaves by hundreds came –
The Chestnuts, Oaks and Maples,
And leaves of every name.
The Sunshine spread a carpet,
And everything was grand,
Miss Weather led the dancing,
Professor Wind the band.

The Chestnuts came in yellow,
The Oaks in crimson dressed;
The lovely Misses Maple
In scarlet looked their best;
All balanced to their partners,
And gaily fluttered by;
The sight was like a rainbow
New fallen from the sky.

Then, in the rustic hollow,
At hide-and-seek they played,
The party closed at sundown,
And everybody stayed.
Professor Wind played louder;
They flew along the ground;
An then the party ended
In a jolly 'hands around'.

*George Cooper*

## Autumn Time

The wind is playing autumn games
Through the gardens and the lanes.
Picking up and swirling round
Leaves of orange, red and brown.

Gusting through each swaying tree,
Tossing apples till they're free.
Shaking conkers till they drop
And open wide with prickly pop.

The wind is dancing full of fun,
Laughing in the autumn sun.
It tumbles acorns, fir cones, leaves,
To make a carpet under trees.

*Anon.*

## A Prayer of Thanks

The leaves go scrunch, scrunch,
Munch, munch,
As we walk through the woods and the parks.
Thank you, God, for the laughing pleasure
Of walking through falling leaves.
Amen.

## Nocturnal Nights

While you are sleeping
So still in your bed
There's a playground of animals
Who love night-time instead.

Out they all come
From their sets and their dens
And greet one another
All nocturnal friends.

The bats like to dance
And the owls like to sing
The hedgehogs run swiftly
Badgers digging for things.

The moths get confused
As they search for the light
The earthworms move slowly
From animals they hide.

It's a playground for nature
That you never will see
Unless you stay up all night
And don't go to sleep.

*Sinéad McNally*

## The Kitten and Falling Leaves

See the Kitten on the wall,
Sporting with the leaves that fall,
Withered leaves – one – two – and three,
From the lofty elder-tree!
Through the calm and frosty air,
Of this morning bright and fair …
 – But the Kitten, how she starts;
Crouches, stretches, paws and darts!
First at one, and then its fellow,
Just as light and just as yellow;
There are many now – now one –
Now they stop and there are none;
What intenseness of desire,
In her upward eye of fire!
With a tiger leap half-way,
Now she meets the coming prey,
Lets it go as fast, and then,
Has it in her power again:
Now she works with three or four,
Like an Indian conjurer;
Quick as he in feats of art,
Far beyond in joy of heart.

*William Wordsworth*

## A Prayer of Thanks

Dear Lord, thank you for pets,
For the special friends we love to play with:
For furry cats and playful dogs,
For hamsters in wheels, and long-eared rabbits.
Help us always to remember to look after them well,
As part of the world you have made.
Amen.

## Blessing

May love and laughter light your days,
and warm your heart and home;
May good and faithful friends be yours,
Wherever you may roam.

### From a Railway Carriage

Faster than fairies, faster than witches,
Bridges and houses, hedges and ditches;
And charging along like troops in a battle,
All through the meadows the horses and cattle:
All of the sights of the hill and the plain
Fly as thick as driving rain;
And ever again, in the wink of an eye,
Painted stations whistle by.

Here is a child who clambers and scrambles,
All by himself and gathering brambles;
Here is a tramp who stands and gazes;
And there is the green for stringing the daisies!
Here is a cart run away in the road
Lumping along with man and load;
And here is a mill and there is a river:
Each a glimpse and gone for ever!

*Robert Louis Stevenson*

## A Prayer

You made the trees
The flowers, the grass,
The moon and stars,
The days that pass.
The creatures, great
And very small
Thank you, God, for all of them. Amen.

## An Irish Blessing

May God grant you always
a sunbeam to warm you,
a moonbeam to charm you,
a sheltering angel
so nothing can harm you,
laughter to cheer you,
faithful friends near you
and, whenever you pray,
heaven to hear you.

*St Patrick*

### The Leprechaun

In a shady nook, one moonlit night, a leprechaun
    I spied
With a scarlet cap and a coat of green, and a
    crúiscín by his side
'Twas 'tic, tac, tic' his hammer went on a tiny shoe
And I laughed to think he was caught at last –
    but the fairy was laughing too.

With tiptoe step and beating heart, quite softly I
    drew nigh
There was mischief in his merry face, a twinkle in
    his eye
He hammered and sang with a tiny voice, and
    drank his mountain dew
Oh, I laughed to think he was caught at last – but
    the fairy was laughing too.

As quick as thought, I seized the elf. 'Your fairy
    purse!' I cried
'The purse I see, is in the hand of that lady by
    your side.'
I turned to look – the elf was gone! Then what was
    I to do?
Oh I laughed to think what a fool I'd been – but
    the fairy was laughing too.

*Robert Dwyer Joyce*

## Sun and Moon

The moon shines clear as silver,
The sun shines bright like gold,
And both are very lovely,
And very, very old.
God hung them up as lanterns,
For all beneath the sky;
And nobody can blow them out,
For they are up too high.

*Charlotte Druitt Cole*

## A Prayer at Bedtime

As I kneel beside my bed
And fold my hands and bow my head,
Dear God, hear this prayer I say:
I want to thank you for today.
Thank you for the sun so bright.
And thank you for the stars tonight;
Thank you for the long hours of happy play;
Thank you for this happy day. Amen.

### Robin Redbreast

Good-bye, good-bye to Summer!
For Summer's nearly done;
The garden smiling faintly,
Cool breezes in the sun;
Our Thrushes now are silent,
Our Swallows flown away, –
But Robin's here, in coat of brown,
With ruddy breast-knot gay.
Robin, Robin Redbreast,
O Robin dear!
Robin singing sweetly
In the falling of the year.

Bright yellow, red, and orange,
The leaves come down in hosts;
The trees are Indian Princes,
But soon they'll turn to Ghosts;
The scanty pears and apples
Hang russet on the bough,
It's Autumn, Autumn, Autumn late,
'Twill soon be Winter now.
Robin, Robin Redbreast,
O Robin dear!
And welaway! my Robin,
For pinching times are near.

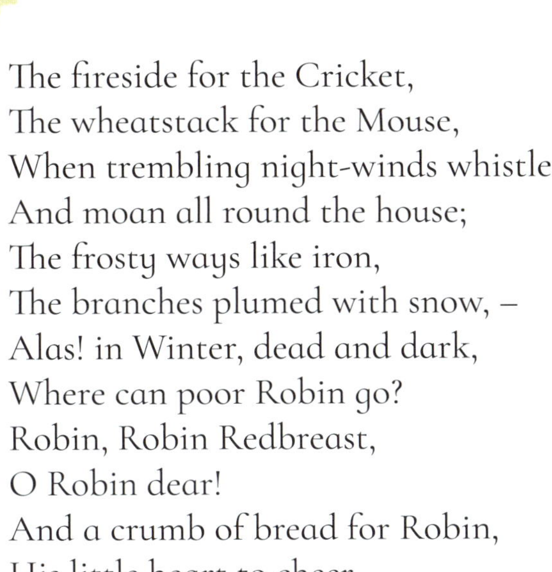

The fireside for the Cricket,
The wheatstack for the Mouse,
When trembling night-winds whistle
And moan all round the house;
The frosty ways like iron,
The branches plumed with snow, –
Alas! in Winter, dead and dark,
Where can poor Robin go?
Robin, Robin Redbreast,
O Robin dear!
And a crumb of bread for Robin,
His little heart to cheer.

*William Allingham*

## Blessing

May the Lord God bless you and keep you.
May the Lord's face shine
Upon you and be glorious to you.
May the Lord turn his face to
You and bring you peace.

**The Night Sky**

All day long
The sun shines bright.
The moon and stars
Come out by night.
From twilight time
They line the skies
And watch the world
With quiet eyes.

*Anon.*

**The Wild Swans at Coole**

The trees are in their autumn beauty,
The woodland paths are dry,
Under the October twilight the water
Mirrors a still sky.

*W.B. Yeats (extract)*

## October Leaves

October leaves are lovely
They rustle when I run.
Sometimes I make a heap
And jump in them for fun.

*Anon.*

## A Prayer of Thanks

Dear Lord, you have given us the changing
seasons, each beautiful in its own way. Thank
you for the wonderful colours that we see all
around us in the autumn.
Amen.

**Psalm 24:1**

The earth is the Lord's and all that is in it,
the world and those who live in it.


**The Fieldmouse**

Where the acorn tumbles down,
Where the ash tree sheds its berry,
With your fur so soft and brown,
With your eye so round and merry,
Scarcely moving the long grass,
Fieldmouse, I can see you pass.

Fieldmouse, fieldmouse, do not go
Where the farmer stacks his treasure,
Find the nut that falls below,
Eat the acorn at your pleasure,
But you must not steal the grain
He has stacked with so much pain.

Make your hole where mosses spring
Underneath the tall oak's shadow,
Pretty, quiet harmless thing,
Play about the sunny meadow.
Keep away from corn and house,
None will harm you, little mouse.

*Cecil Frances Alexander*

## A Prayer

May God bless us at the first light of dawn when
the new day begins and when the long day is
over and we snuggle down in our bed.
Amen.


## Duilleoga Deasa

Duilleoga deasa buí.
Duilleoga deasa deasa,
Ag damhsa ar an gcraobh.

Duilleoga deasa deasa,
Duilleoga deasa buí.
Duilleoga deasa deasa,
Ag imeacht leis an ngaoth.

Duilleoga deasa deasa,
Duilleoga deasa buí.
Duilleoga deasa deasa,
Ar an talamh ina luí.

*Traditional*

# November

It's November and the clocks have changed, plunging us into longer, darker evenings. The skies are grey and seem to be sitting on our heads, and we have to button up our coats against the wind and rain. At night we can sit by a blazing fire, seeing pictures in the flames.

**A Prayer**

When we go home tonight,
the sky will be getting dark,
Everything will be dreary and dull …
On the dark, dark evenings, Lord, give us light hearts,
So that even in darkness we can see beauty. Amen.

**Psalm 147:16–18**

He gives snow like wool;
He scatters frost like ashes.
He hurls down hail like crumbs –
who can stand before his cold?
He sends out his words, and melts them;
He makes his wind blow, and the waters flow.

# SAMHAIN

**November**

When autumn comes, the poets sing a dirge:
The year must perish; all the flowers are dead;
The sheaves are gathered; and the mottled quail
Runs in the stubble, but the lark has fled!

Still, autumn ushers in the Christmas cheer,
The holly-berries and the ivy-tree:
They weave a chaplet for the Old Year's bier,
These waiting mourners do not sing for me!

 I find sweet peace in depths of autumn woods,
Where grow the ragged ferns and roughened moss;
The naked, silent trees have taught me this, –
The loss of beauty is not always loss!

*Elizabeth Drew Stoddard*

## Courage

Courage! What if the snows are deep,
And what if the hills are long and steep,
And the days are short and the nights are long,
And the good are weak and the bad are strong.
Courage! The snow is a field of play,
And the longest hill has a well-worn way,
There are songs that shorten the longest night,
There's a day when wrong shall be ruled right,
So courage! Courage! 'Tis never so far
From a plodded path to a shining star.

*Anon.*

## The Elf Singing

An Elf sat on a twig,
He was not very big,
He sang a little song,
He did not think it wrong;
But he was on a Wizard's ground,
Who hated all sweet sound.

Elf, Elf,
Take care of yourself.
He's coming behind you,
To seize you and bind you
And stifle your song.

The Elf went on with his song,
It grew more clear and strong;
It lifted him into air,
He floated singing away,
With rainbows in his hair.

*William Allingham*

## A Prayer

Soft, pale moonlight bathes our world -
And all is very, very quiet.
Dear Lord, let your peace be in our minds
As softly as the moonlight. Amen.

## A Blessing Prayer

May God bless us
In our work and in our play each day.
May God bless us
In our smiles and in our tears.
May God bless us
In our successes and in our disappointments.
May God bless us through each day and
through each night. Amen.


## A Winter Poem

I wonder if the snow loves the tree and fields,
that it kisses them gently?
And then it covers them up snug, you know,
with a white quilt;
perhaps it says 'Go to sleep darlings,
till the summer comes again.'

*Lewis Carroll*

### Down by the Salley Gardens

Down by the salley gardens
my love and I did meet;
She passed the salley gardens
with little snow-white feet.
She bid me take love easy,
as the leaves grow on the tree;
But I, being young and foolish,
with her would not agree.
In a field by the river
my love and I did stand,
And on my leaning shoulder
She laid her snow-white hand.
She bid me take life easy,
as the grass grows on the weirs;
But I was young and foolish,
and now am full of tears.

*W.B. Yeats*

## Winter-Time

Late lies the wintry sun a-bed,
A frosty, fiery sleepy-head;
Blinks but an hour or two; and then,
A blood-red orange, sets again.

Close by the jolly fire I sit
To warm my frozen bones a bit;
Or with a reindeer-sled, explore
The colder countries round the door.

Black are my steps on silver sod;
Thick blows my frosty breath abroad;
And tree and house, and hill and lake,
Are frosted like a wedding-cake.

*Robert Louis Stevenson*

## Beannacht

Slán agus beannacht.

## The Arrow and the Song

I shot an arrow into the air,
It fell to earth, I knew not where;
For, so swiftly it flew, the sight
Could not follow it in its flight.

I breathed a song into the air,
It fell to earth, I knew not where;
For who has sight so keen and strong,
That it can follow the flight of song?

Long, long afterward, in an oak
I found the arrow, still unbroke;
And the song, from beginning to end,
I found again in the heart of a friend.

*Henry Wadsworth Longfellow*


## An Evening Prayer

Before the end of the day,
Creator of the world, we pray
That you, with steadfast love, would keep
Your watch around us while we sleep.
From evil dreams defend our sight;
From fears and terrors of the night. Amen.

## A Prayer

May the peace of God,
which passes all understanding,
Keep our hearts and minds
In the knowledge and love of God,
And of his Son Jesus Christ our Lord,
And the blessing of God almighty,
The Father, the Son and the Holy Spirit,
Be with us and remain with us always. Amen.

## The Wind

The wind stood up and gave a shout.
He whistled on his fingers and
Kicked the withered leaves about
And thumped the branches with his hand.

*James Stephens (extract)*

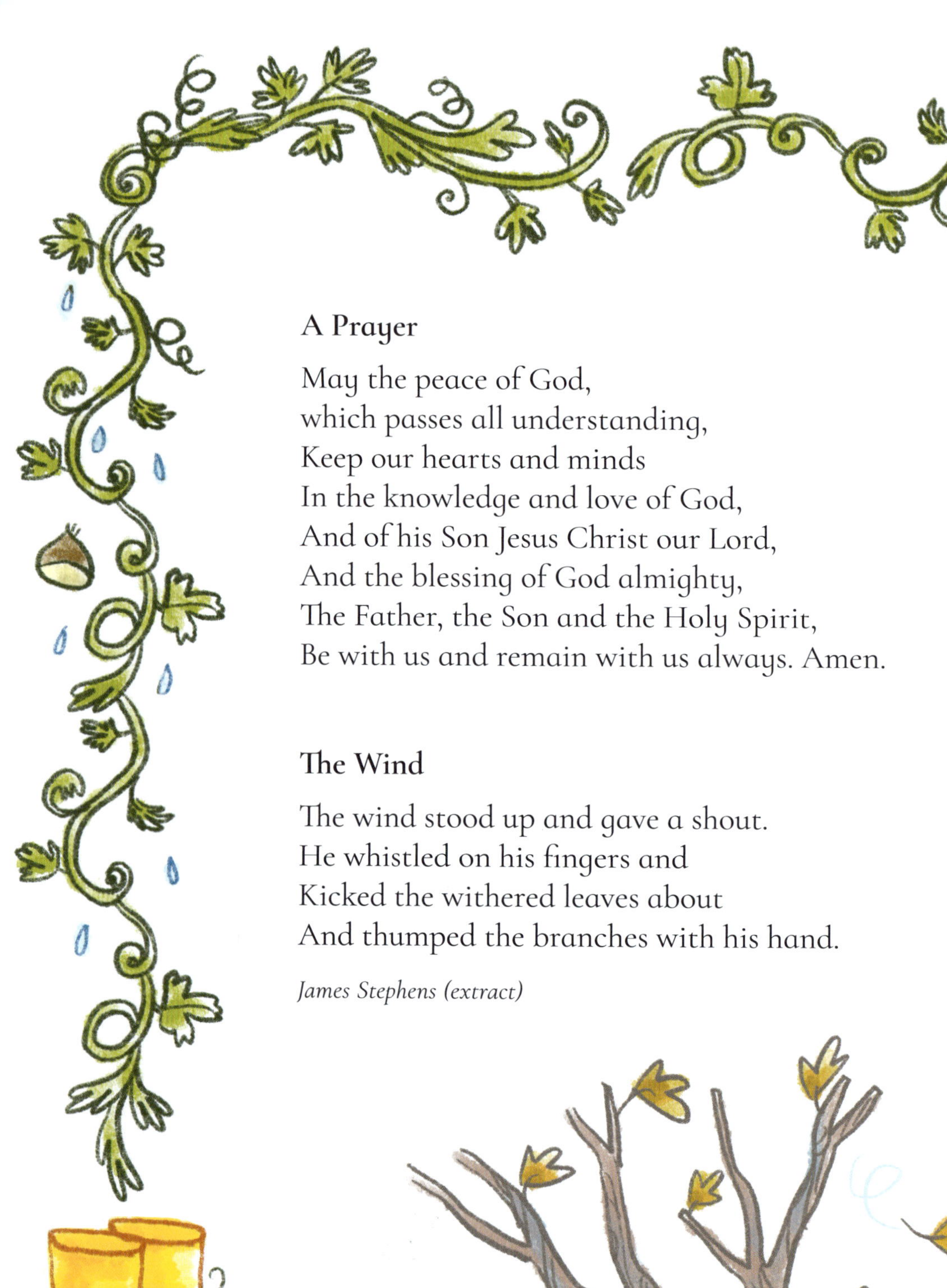

## Snow-Flakes

Out of the bosom of the Air,
Out of the cloud-folds of her garments shaken,
Over the woodlands brown and bare,
Over the harvest-fields forsaken,
Silent, and soft, and slow
Descends the snow.

*Henry Wadsworth Longfellow*


## Blessing

May you always be blessed
With walls for the wind,
A roof for the rain,
A warm cup of tea by the fire.
Laughter to cheer you,
Those you love near you,
And all that your heart might desire.

### A Prayer of Thanks

Lord, I can skip and jump and shout and SING!
I can skip and clap and stamp and SWING!
Thank you for making me alive!
Amen.


### A Classroom Prayer

We have hung our coats on their pegs –
The classroom has a special winter smell.
Thank you, God, for the warmth and comfort of our school;
Bless those who look after it.
May it always be a place of welcome
And safety for children.
Amen.

## Picture-Books in Winter

Summer fading, winter comes –
Frosty mornings, tingling thumbs,
Window robins, winter rooks,
And the picture story-books.
Water now is turned to stone
Nurse and I can walk upon;
Still we find the flowing brooks
In the picture story-books.
All the pretty things put by,
Wait upon the children's eye,
Sheep and shepherds, trees and crooks,
In the picture story-books.
We may see how all things are
Seas and cities, near and far,
And the flying fairies' looks,
In the picture story-books.
How am I to sing your praise,
Happy chimney-corner days,
Sitting safe in nursery nooks,
Reading picture story-books?

*Robert Louis Stevenson*

## November Morning

A tingling, misty marvel
Blew hither in the night,
And now the little peach-trees
Are clasped in frozen light.
Upon the apple-branches
An icy film is caught,
With trailing threads of gossamer
In pearly patterns wrought.
The autumn sun, in wonder,
Is gayly peering through
This silver-tissued network
Across the frosty blue.
The weather-vane is fire-tipped,
The honeysuckle shows
A dazzling icy splendour,
And crystal is the rose.
Around the eaves are fringes
Of icicles that seem
To mock the summer rainbows
With many-colored gleam.
Along the walk, the pebbles
Are each a precious stone;
The grass is tasselled hoarfrost,
The clover jewel-sown.
Such sparkle, sparkle, sparkle
Fills all the frosty air,
Oh, can it be that darkness
Is ever anywhere!

*Evaleen Stein*

## All in All

I saw the moon in the morning
Shining low down in the west,
The stars shut up their blossoms
The earth, the sky at rest.
The trees, like children waiting,
Stood silent in a row,
The shadows cast by moonlight
Were moving to and fro.

I gazed upon the river
That seemed to run so slow;
Then came the golden daylight
And made the moon to go.
The dreamy river dimpled,
The shadows passed away,
And all the waiting children
Were happy with the day.

*George William Russell (A.E.)*

## November

The leaves are fading and falling,
The winds are rough and wild,
The birds have ceased their calling,
But let me tell you my child,

Through day by day, as it closes,
Doth darker and colder grow,
The roots of the bright red roses
Will keep alive in the snow.

And when the winter is over,
The boughs will get new leaves,
The quail will come back to the clover,
And the swallow back to the eaves.

The robin will wear on his bosom
A vest that is bright and new,
And the loveliest way-side blossom
Will shine with the sun and dew.

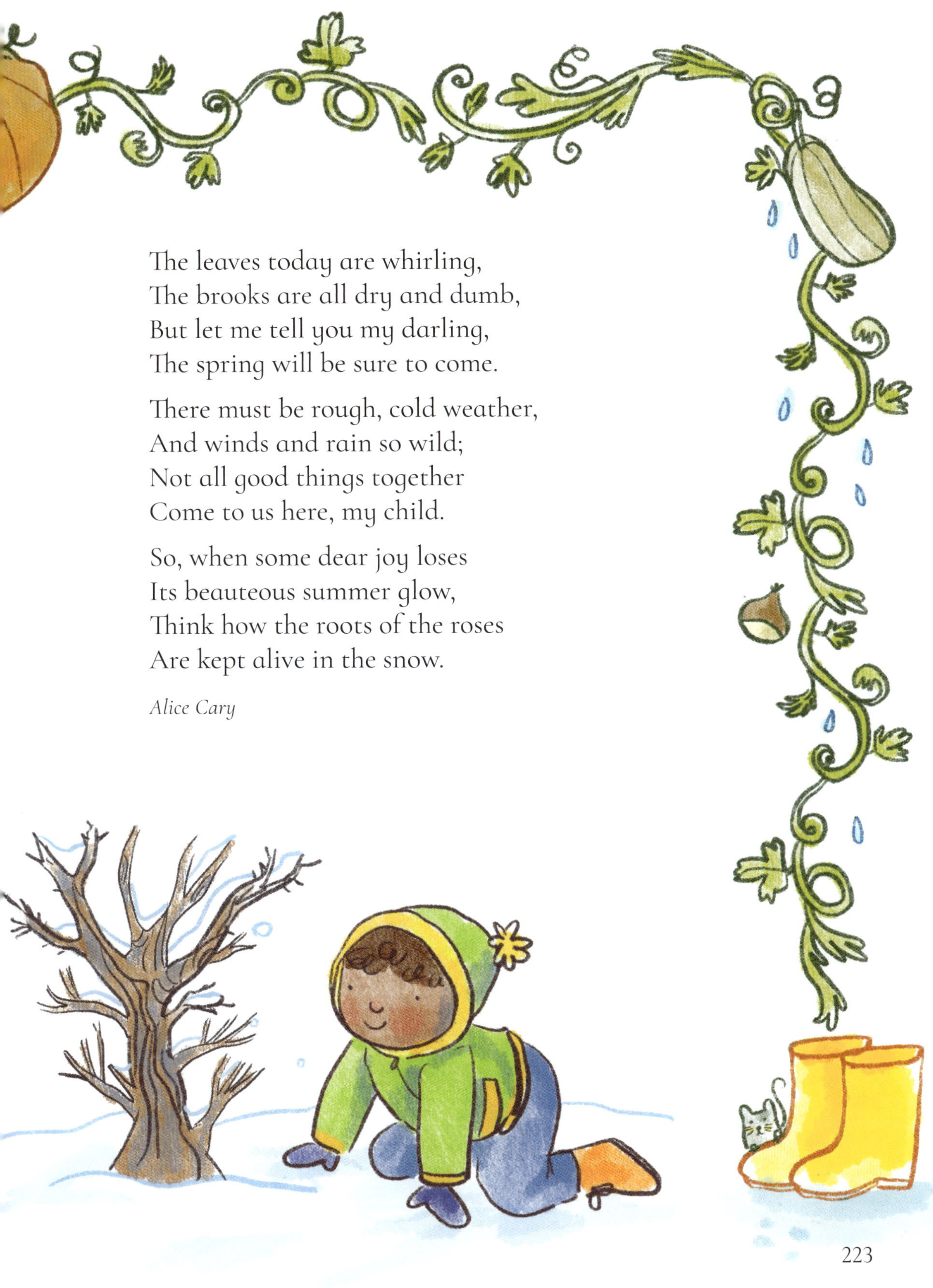

The leaves today are whirling,
The brooks are all dry and dumb,
But let me tell you my darling,
The spring will be sure to come.

There must be rough, cold weather,
And winds and rain so wild;
Not all good things together
Come to us here, my child.

So, when some dear joy loses
Its beauteous summer glow,
Think how the roots of the roses
Are kept alive in the snow.

*Alice Cary*

**I Have News for You**

I have news for you
The stag bells, winter snows, summer is gone.
Wind high and cold, the sun low, short its course
The sea running high.
Deep red the bracken, its shape is lost
The wild goose has raised its accustomed cry
Cold has seized the birds' wings
Season of ice
This is my news.

*Anon.*

**Mise Raifteirí an File**

Is mise Raifteirí an file,
lán dóchais is grá,
Le súile gan solas,
le ciúnas gan chrá
Ag dul siar ar m'aistear
Le solas mo chroí
Fann agus tuirseach
Go deireadh mo shlí
Féach anois mé
Is mo chúl le balla
Ag seinm ceoil
Do phócaí folmha.

*Antoine Ó Raifteirí*

## A Gaelic Blessing

Deep peace of the running wave to you
Deep peace of the flowing air to you
Deep peace of the quiet earth to you
Deep peace of the shining stars to you
Deep peace of the gentle night to you
Moon and stars pour their healing light on you.

## Altú tar éis Bia

Go raibh maith agat, a Dhia,
Go raibh maith agat don bhia.
Go raibh maith agat, a Dhia.
Áiméan.

## The Cold Earth Slept Below

The cold earth slept below;
Above the cold sky shone;
And all around,
With a chilling sound,
From caves of ice and fields of snow
The breath of night like death did flow
Beneath the sinking moon.

The wintry hedge was black;
The green grass was not seen;
The birds did rest
On the bare thorn's breast,
Whose roots, beside the pathway track,
Had bound their folds o'er many a crack
Which the frost had made between.

*Percy Bysshe Shelley*

## Star Light, Star Bright

Star light, star bright,
First star I see tonight,
I wish I may, I wish I might,
Have this wish I wish tonight.

*Anon.*


## Grace before Meals

God is great,
And God is good,
We thank him
For this food.

By his hand
Must all be fed:
Thanks be to God
For daily bread. Amen.

# December

The days are getting shorter and colder, all the plants in the gardens and parks are nipped by frost and it seems as if we'll never see the spring. But ... Christmas is coming! While we wait impatiently for all the good things this brings, the four weeks of Advent will help us to prepare everything we need for this special time of year.

**A Prayer when Lighting the Advent Candles**

Shine on us, dear Lord;
Guide our path through the dark of night;
Come to us, O Christ the Light.
Amen.

# NOLLAIG

**Snow-Bound – A Winter Idyl**

Unwarmed by any sunset light
The grey day darkened into night,
A night made hoary with the swarm
And whirl-dance of the blinding storm,
As zigzag, wavering to and fro,
Crossed and recrossed the wingèd snow:
And ere the early bedtime came
The white drift piled the window-frame,
And through the glass the clothes-line posts
Looked in like tall and sheeted ghosts.

*John Greenleaf Whittier*

### The First Sleigh-Ride

O happy time of fleecy rime
And falling flakes, and O
The glad surprise in the baby eyes
That never saw the snow!
Down shining ways the flying sleighs
Go jingling by, and see!
Beside the gate, the horses wait
And neigh for you and me!

*Evaleen Stein*

### Snowman

'Snowman, have you chilblains,
Standing in the snow ?'
'Child, I can't get chilblains,
On finger or on toe.'

*Winifred M. Letts*

### Blessing

Faith makes all things possible;
Hope makes all things work;
Love makes everything beautiful.
May you have all three and more.

230

## The Frost

The Frost looked forth, one still, clear night,
And he said, 'Now I shall be out of sight;
So through the valley and over the height
In silence I'll take my way.
I will not go like that blustering train,
The wind and the snow, the hail and the rain,
Who make so much bustle and noise in vain,
But I'll be as busy as they!'

Then he went to the mountain, and powdered its crest,
He climbed up the trees, and their boughs he dressed
With diamonds and pearls, and over the breast
Of the quivering lake he spread
A coat of mail, that it need not fear
The downward point of many a spear
That he hung on its margin, far and near,
Where a rock could rear its head.

He went to the windows of those who slept,
And over each pane like a fairy crept;
Wherever he breathed, wherever he stepped,
By the light of the moon were seen
Most beautiful things. There were flowers and trees,
There were bevies of birds and swarms of bees,
There were cities, thrones, temples, and towers, and these
All pictured in silver sheen!

*Hannah Flagg Gould*

### A Prayer of Thanks

Dear Lord,
Thank you for all the love that surrounds us
every day and takes us into the peace of the night.
Amen.


### Is é do bheatha, a Mhuire

Is é do bheatha, a Mhuire,
atá lán de ghrásta, tá an Tiarna leat.
Is beannaithe thú idir mhná
Agus is beannaithe toradh do bhroinne, Íosa.
A Naomh Mhuire, a mháthair Dé,
guigh orainn na peacaigh,
Anois is ar uair ar mbáis. Áiméan.

232

## Christmas Star

A diamond shines no brighter
Than that lovely Christmas star.
It shines in all its brilliance;
It's seen from near or far.

A symbol of the Christ child
As He lay upon the hay,
It tells to all the waiting world
A King was born that day.

O Bethlehem Star, keep shining,
Give us faith and hope and love,
Keep our thoughts forever turning
To the Saviour up above.

Give us strength and hope and courage
To do our best by far
And never falter in our faith
As we watch that Christmas star.

*Anon.*

## The Bells

Hear the sledges with the bells –
Silver bells!
What a world of merriment their melody foretells!
How they tinkle, tinkle, tinkle,
In the icy air of night!
While the stars, that oversprinkle
All the heavens, seem to twinkle
With a crystalline delight;
Keeping time, time, time,
In a sort of Runic rhyme,
To the tintinnabulation that so musically wells
From the bells, bells, bells, bells –
Bells, bells, bells –
From the jingling and the tinkling of the bells.

*Edgar Allan Poe*


## Christmas Hearth

A full moon and the shadows of bare trees,
On fallen snow that blurs the gravel path
How good the silver world inside I see
The colour of kind thoughts about the hearth
The draw no curtain, let the lone moon see
The fire and our warm tranquility.

*Winifred M. Letts*

**The Miracle of Friendship**

There is a Miracle called Friendship
that dwells within the heart
and you don't know how it happens
or when it even starts.
But the happiness it brings you
always gives a special lift
and you realise that friendship is
God's most precious gift.

*Jean Kyler McManus*


**A Prayer of Thanks**

Dear Lord,
thank you for warm bright fires on
cold winter nights.
Amen.

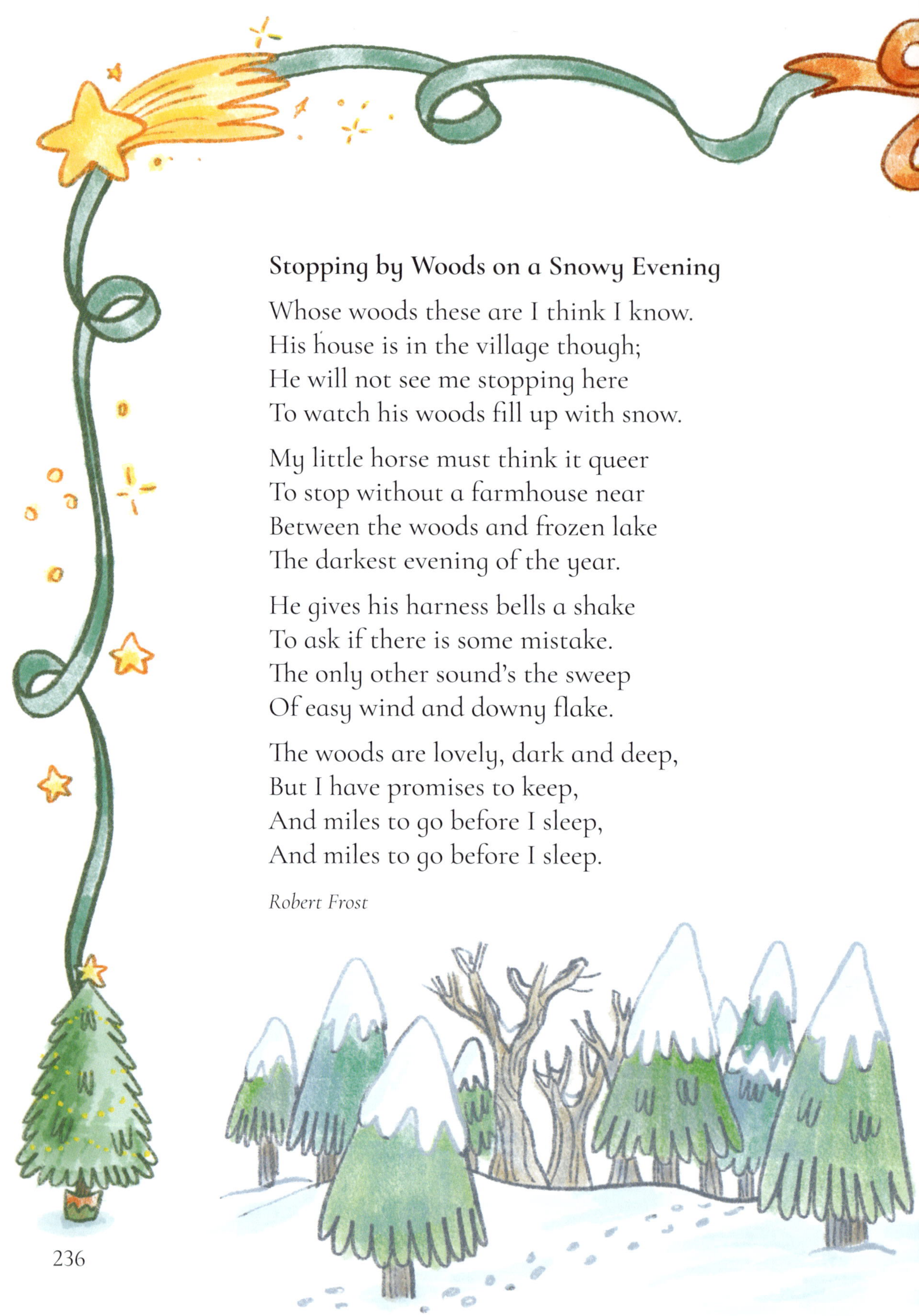

**Stopping by Woods on a Snowy Evening**

Whose woods these are I think I know.
His house is in the village though;
He will not see me stopping here
To watch his woods fill up with snow.

My little horse must think it queer
To stop without a farmhouse near
Between the woods and frozen lake
The darkest evening of the year.

He gives his harness bells a shake
To ask if there is some mistake.
The only other sound's the sweep
Of easy wind and downy flake.

The woods are lovely, dark and deep,
But I have promises to keep,
And miles to go before I sleep,
And miles to go before I sleep.

*Robert Frost*

**Blessing for Christmas**

God grant you lightness in your step,
A smile on every face you meet,
Loved ones gathered at your hearth,
And at your door, good friends to greet
A holy hymn upon your lips,
A window candle burning bright
And may the Good Lord bless your heart
And come to dwell here Christmas night.


**A Prayer of Thanks**

Dear Jesus, thank you for my family, my parents,
my granny and grandad, my brothers and sisters,
my uncles and aunts and my cousins. Help me to
be kind to them.
Amen.

### Valparaiso

Tháinig long ó Valparaiso
Scaoileadh téad a seol sa chuan.
Chuir a hainm dom i gcuimhne
Ríocht na Gréine, Tír na mBua.

'Gluais,' ar sí, 'ar thuras fada
Liom ó scamall is ó cheo,
Tá fé shleasaibh gorm Andes
Cathair scáfar, glé mar sheod.'

Bhíos óg is ní imeoinnse,
Am an dóchais, tús mo shaoil,
Chreideas fós go raibh i ndán dom
Iontaisí na ndán 's na scéal.

Ghluais an long thar lintibh mara
Fad ó shin is a crann mar ór,
Scríobh a scéal ar phár na hoíche,
Ard i rian na réaltann mór.

Fillfidh sí aris chugam áfach;
Chífead cathair bhán fén sléibh,
Le hais mara na síochána –
Creidim fós beagnach, a Dhé.

*Pádraig de Brún*

238

## Granny

Through every nook and every cranny
The wind blew in on poor old Granny
Around her knees, into each ear
(And up her nose as well, I fear)

All through the night the wind grew worse
It nearly made the vicar curse
The top had fallen off the steeple
Just missing him (and other people)

It blew on man, it blew on beast
It blew on nun, it blew on priest
It blew the wig off Auntie Fanny –
But most of all, it blew on Granny!

*Spike Milligan*

## December

All through the year
As the months go past
Each is like a friend
December is the last.
December is the best month,
We love to see it come
With all the lovely things it brings
Like Christmas and good fun.

*Anon.*

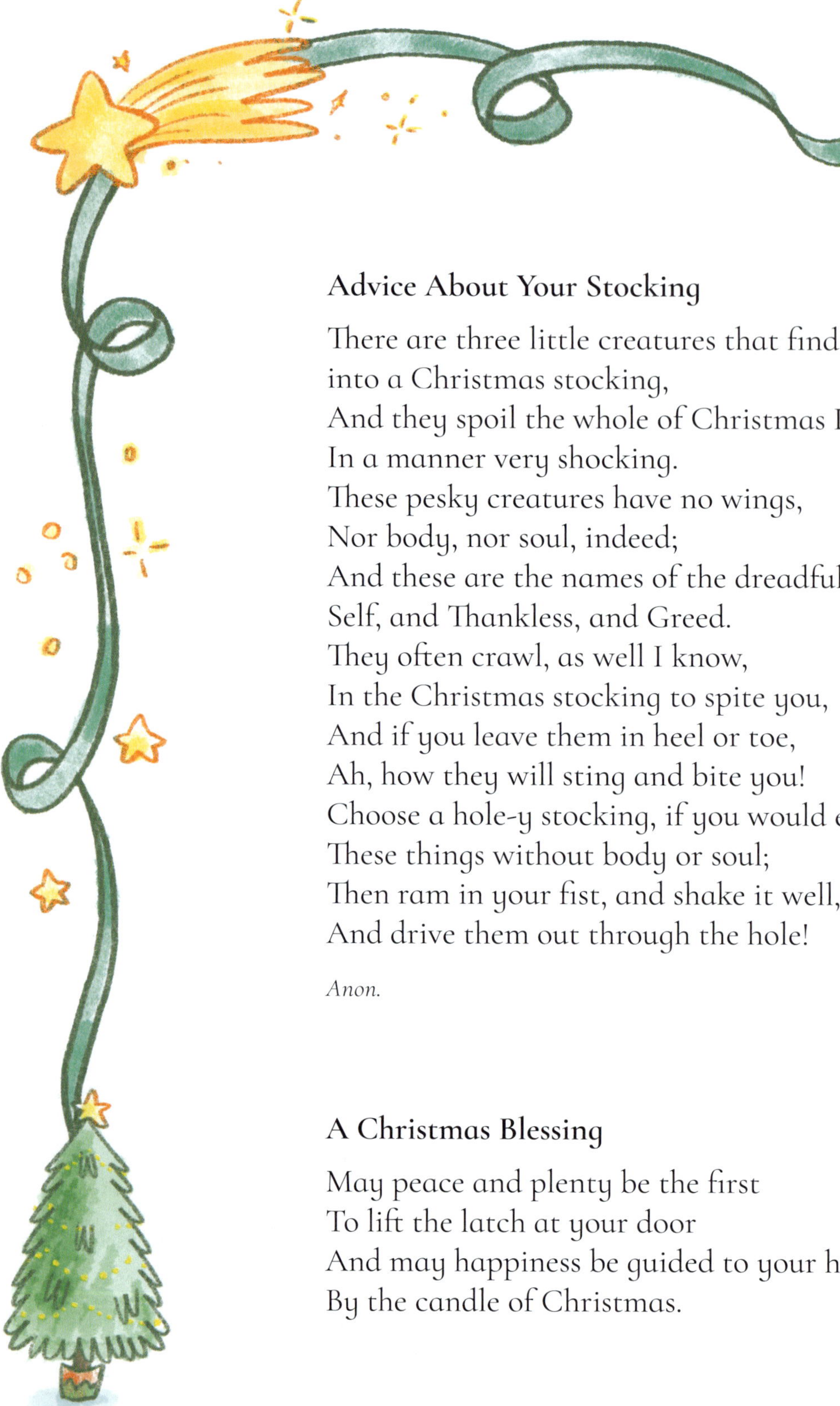

## Advice About Your Stocking

There are three little creatures that find their way
into a Christmas stocking,
And they spoil the whole of Christmas Day
In a manner very shocking.
These pesky creatures have no wings,
Nor body, nor soul, indeed;
And these are the names of the dreadful things, –
Self, and Thankless, and Greed.
They often crawl, as well I know,
In the Christmas stocking to spite you,
And if you leave them in heel or toe,
Ah, how they will sting and bite you!
Choose a hole-y stocking, if you would expel
These things without body or soul;
Then ram in your fist, and shake it well,
And drive them out through the hole!

*Anon.*


## A Christmas Blessing

May peace and plenty be the first
To lift the latch at your door
And may happiness be guided to your home
By the candle of Christmas.

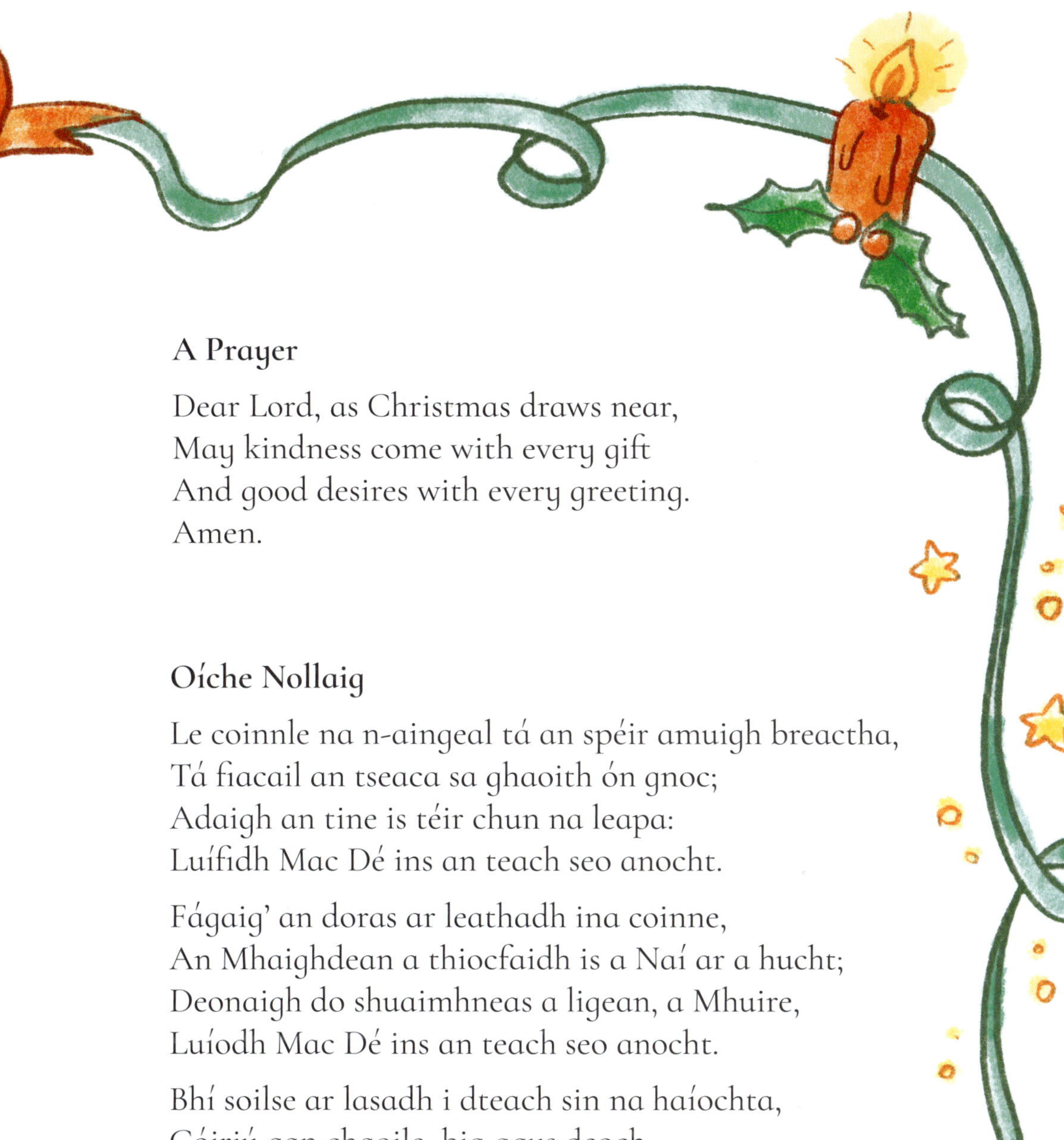

## A Prayer

Dear Lord, as Christmas draws near,
May kindness come with every gift
And good desires with every greeting.
Amen.


## Oíche Nollaig

Le coinnle na n-aingeal tá an spéir amuigh breactha,
Tá fiacail an tseaca sa ghaoith ón gnoc;
Adaigh an tine is téir chun na leapa:
Luífidh Mac Dé ins an teach seo anocht.

Fágaig' an doras ar leathadh ina coinne,
An Mhaighdean a thiocfaidh is a Naí ar a hucht;
Deonaigh do shuaimhneas a ligean, a Mhuire,
Luíodh Mac Dé ins an teach seo anocht.

Bhí soilse ar lasadh i dteach sin na haíochta,
Cóiriú gan chaoile, bia agus deoch,
Do cheannaithe olla, do cheannaithe síoda
Ach luífidh Mac Dé ins an teach seo anocht.

*Máire Mhac an tSaoi*


## Beannacht

Saol fada agus breacshláinte chugat.

## A Visit from St Nicholas

'Twas the night before Christmas, when all through
the house
Not a creature was stirring, not even a mouse;
The stockings were hung by the chimney with care,
In hopes that St Nicholas soon would be there;
The children were nestled all snug in their beds;
While visions of sugar-plums danced in their heads;
Down the chimney St Nicholas came with a bound.
He was dressed all in fur, from his head to his foot,
And his clothes were all tarnished with ashes
  and soot;
A bundle of toys he had flung on his back,
And he looked like a peddler just opening his pack.
He spoke not a word, but went straight to his work,
And filled all the stockings; then turned with a jerk,
And laying his finger aside of his nose,
And giving a nod, up the chimney he rose;
He sprang to his sleigh, to his team gave a whistle,
And away they all flew like the down of a thistle.
But I heard him exclaim, ere he drove out of sight –
'Happy Christmas to all, and to all a good night!'

*Clement Clarke Moore (extract)*

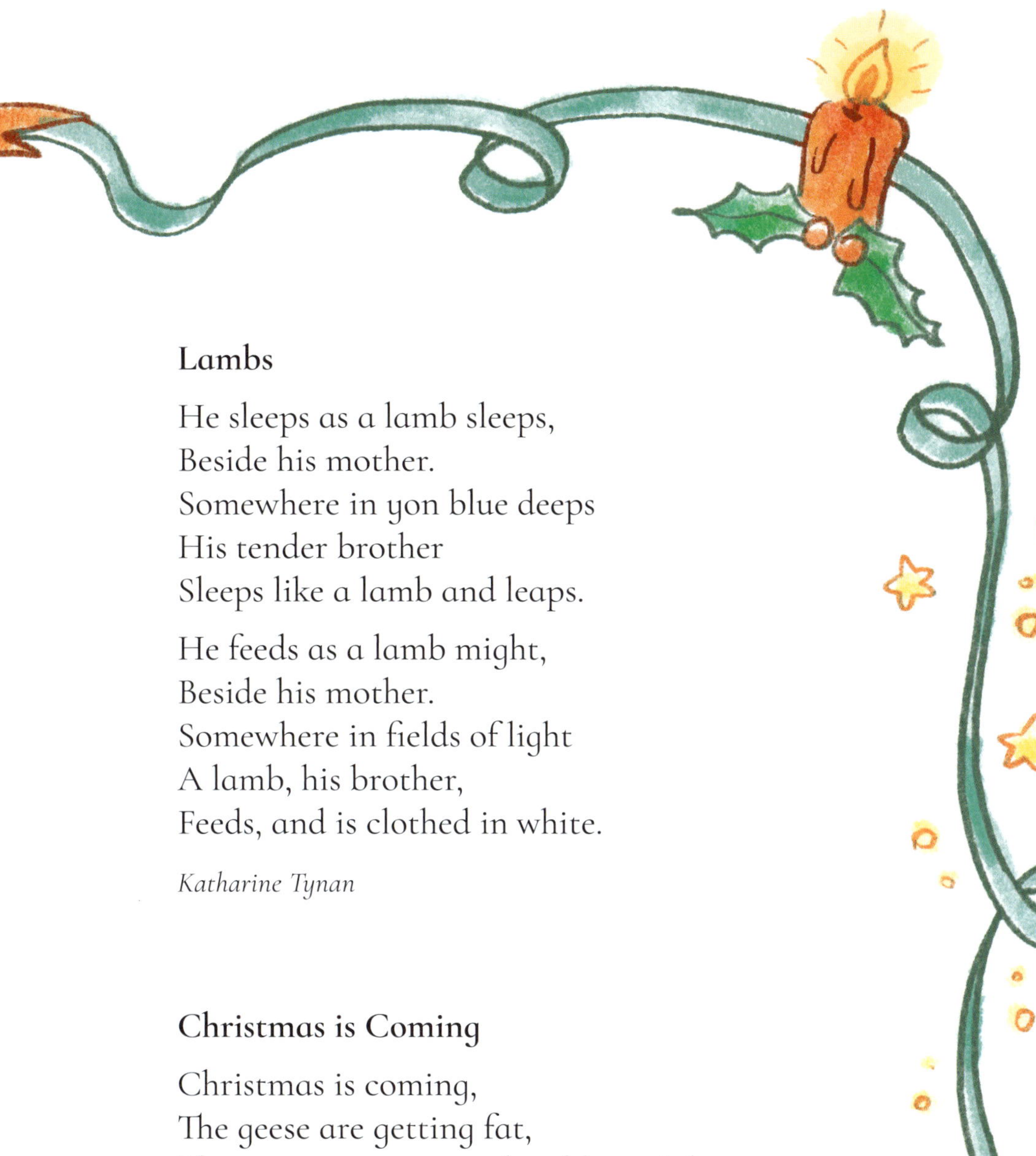

## Lambs

He sleeps as a lamb sleeps,
Beside his mother.
Somewhere in yon blue deeps
His tender brother
Sleeps like a lamb and leaps.

He feeds as a lamb might,
Beside his mother.
Somewhere in fields of light
A lamb, his brother,
Feeds, and is clothed in white.

*Katharine Tynan*


## Christmas is Coming

Christmas is coming,
The geese are getting fat,
Please put a penny in the old man's hat.
If you haven't got a penny,
A ha'penny will do,
If you haven't got a ha'penny,
Then God bless you.

*Anon.*

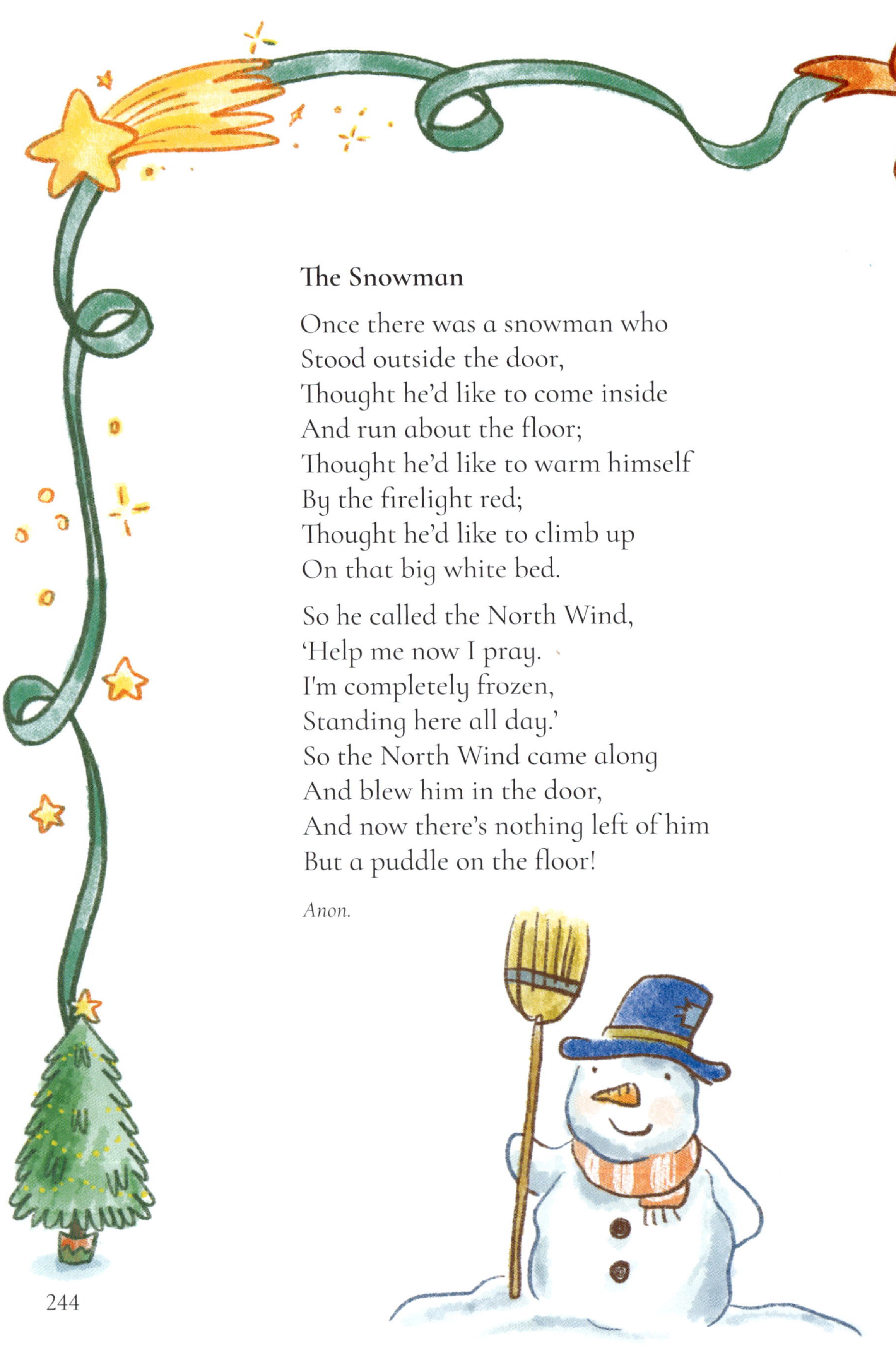

### The Snowman

Once there was a snowman who
Stood outside the door,
Thought he'd like to come inside
And run about the floor;
Thought he'd like to warm himself
By the firelight red;
Thought he'd like to climb up
On that big white bed.

So he called the North Wind,
'Help me now I pray.
I'm completely frozen,
Standing here all day.'
So the North Wind came along
And blew him in the door,
And now there's nothing left of him
But a puddle on the floor!

*Anon.*

## Christmas Carol

The kings they came from out the south,
All dressed in ermine fine;
They bore Him gold and chrysoprase,
And gifts of precious wine.
The shepherds came from out the north,
Their coats were brown and old;
They brought Him little new-born lambs –
They had not any gold.
The wise men came from out the east,
And they were wrapped in white;
The star that led them all the way
Did glorify the night.
The angels came from heaven high,
And they were clad with wings;
And lo, they brought a joyful song
The host of heaven sings.
The kings they knocked upon the door,
The wise men entered in,
The shepherds followed after them
To hear the song begin.
The angels sang through all the night
Until the rising sun,
But little Jesus fell asleep
Before the song was done.

*Sara Teasdale*

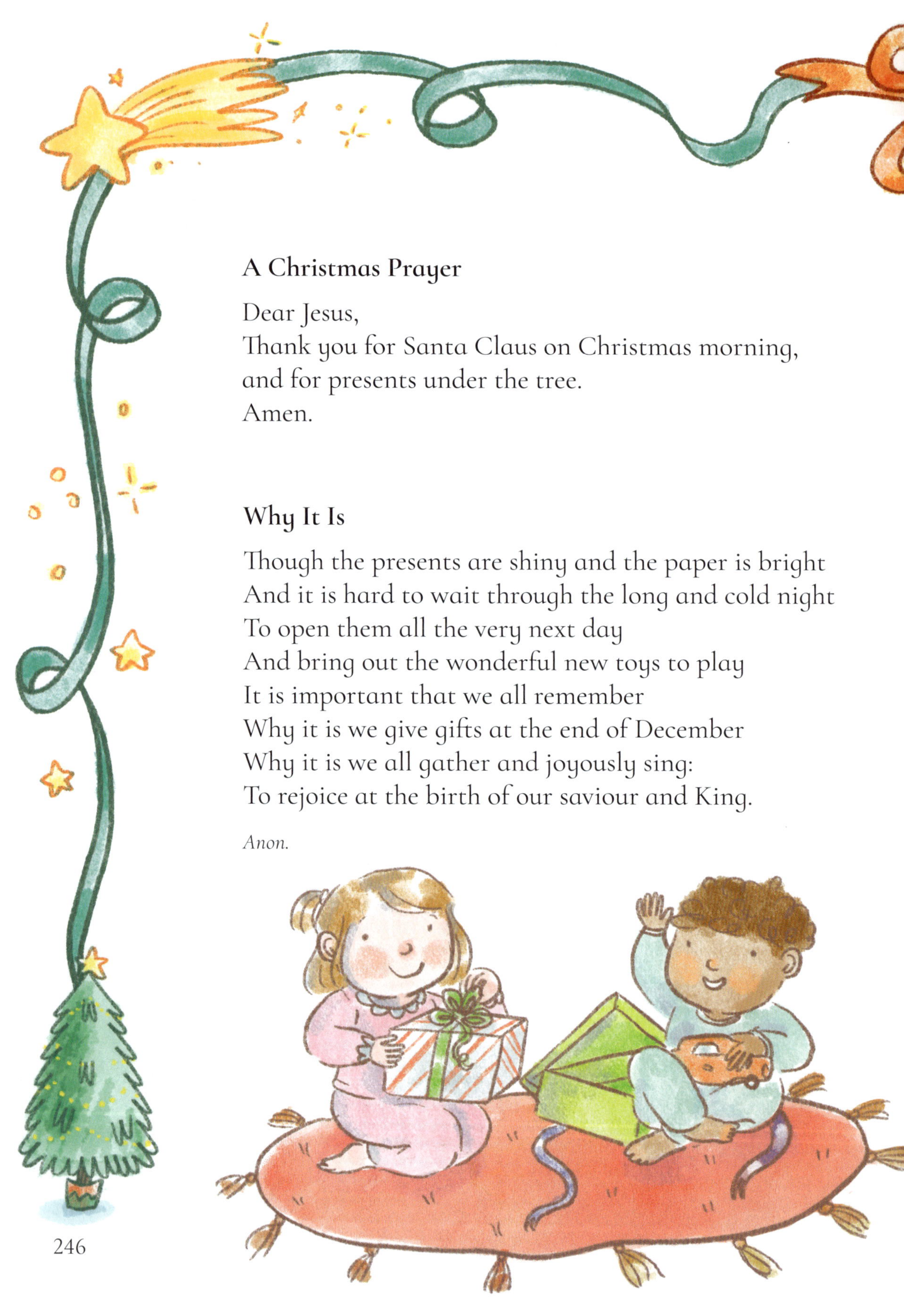

**A Christmas Prayer**

Dear Jesus,
Thank you for Santa Claus on Christmas morning,
and for presents under the tree.
Amen.


**Why It Is**

Though the presents are shiny and the paper is bright
And it is hard to wait through the long and cold night
To open them all the very next day
And bring out the wonderful new toys to play
It is important that we all remember
Why it is we give gifts at the end of December
Why it is we all gather and joyously sing:
To rejoice at the birth of our saviour and King.

*Anon.*

A Prayer of Thanks

Thank you, God, for the world so bright,
For the moon and all the stars at night.
Amen.


A Prayer of Thanks

Lord Jesus,
You were a tiny baby
In a manger,
In Bethlehem.
You grew up to be a man
Who helped people who were ill,
Or sad, or lonely,
And you showed us how to love
Other people as God does.
Thank you, Lord Jesus. Amen.

# PRAYERS FOR SPECIAL OCCASIONS

**A Birthday Prayer**

Dear Jesus,
Today is my birthday. Thank you for this special day,
and thank you for keeping me safe all year. Bless my
parents, teachers and friends, who make my life so
happy. Amen.

**A Prayer for the First Day at School**

Dear Jesus,
This is the beginning of the school year and I'm
excited, but I'm a bit nervous as well, because I will
be meeting new friends and new teachers. Whenever I
am worried help me to remember that you are always
by my side. Amen.

**Paidir roimh Chomaoineach**

A Thiarna Íosa, tar chugam.
A Thiarna Íosa, tabhair dom do ghrá.
A Thiarna Íosa, tar chugam agus tabhair tú féin dom.
A Thiarna Íosa, a chara na bpáistí, tar chugam.
A Thiarna Íosa, is tú mo Thiarna agus mo Dhia.
Moladh leat, a Thiarna Íosa Críost. Áiméan.

# Paidreacha ar Ócáidí Speisialta

**A Prayer before First Communion**

Lord Jesus, come to me, Lord Jesus, give me your love. Be near me, Lord Jesus. I ask you to stay close by me forever and love me. Bless all of us children in your loving care and take us to heaven to live with you there. Amen.

**A First Communion Day Prayer**

I kneel and pray on this,
my First Communion Day.
Dear Jesus, watch me grow,
and teach me all I need to know
Fill my heart with joy each day,
and if I ever lose my way,
Guide me back –
for this I pray. Amen.

**A Prayer before Going on Holiday**

Dear God, we are going on holiday today.
Bless us with a safe journey and sunny weather.
Help me not to fight too much with my brothers
and sisters and not to argue with my parents, so
that we can all have a good time. Amen.

## A Prayer to Welcome a New Baby Brother

Dear Jesus, thank for the special gift of my new baby brother. I'm glad you sent him to our family. Help me to look after him and be a good example to him in everything I do. Please make me patient when he is crying. Amen.

## A Prayer to Welcome a New Baby Sister

Dear Jesus, thank for the special gift of my new baby sister. I'm glad you sent her to our family. Help me to look after her and be a good example to her in everything I do. Please make me patient when she is crying. Amen.

## A Christmas Prayer

Dear God,
Thank you for Jesus, who came down from heaven to be with us. It's his birthday today. Thank you for my family, who work so hard to look after me and give me everything I need. And thank you for the toys and presents that Santa brought. Amen.

## A Christmas Grace before Meals

Dear God, thank you for this wonderful Christmas dinner. Bless all the people who have brought it to the table – the farmers, the shopkeepers and the cook. Thank you for families and friends and the wonderful world that we live in. Amen.

## An Easter Prayer

This is a very special Sunday, the most important Sunday of the year. Thank you, God, for all the love you give us and for the gift of your son Jesus. Amen.

## An Easter Prayer

Dear Jesus, the Easter Bunny who brings us our lovely chocolate eggs reminds us of all the animals you have made. Thank you for your beautiful Creation. Amen.

## An Easter Grace before Meals

Dear Lord, this Easter Sunday we are celebrating Jesus rising from the dead. As we sit down to this lovely meal, we remember all those people who have nothing to eat today. Bless us and this food. Amen.

# Biographies • Beathaisnéisí

**Alexander, Cecil Frances** (1818–1895), Anglo-Irish hymn-writer and poet, was born in Dublin. When she was 15, she moved to Strabane and lived in Ulster for the rest of her life. She published her very popular *Hymns for Little Children* in 1848, which contained the perennial favourite, 'All Things Bright and Beautiful'.

**Allingham, William** (1824–1889), Irish poet, diarist and editor, was born in Ballyshannon, County Donegal. He published several collections of poetry – one of his best-known poems is 'The Fairies'.

**Anon.** Throughout history, many significant works of poetry have been attributed to anonymous authors. These poets have contributed richly to various literary traditions.

**Bernardone, Giovanni di Pietro di** (c. 1181–1226), better known as **St Francis of Assisi,** was an Italian mystic, poet and Catholic friar who founded the religious order of the Franciscans. Inspired to lead a Christian life of poverty, he became a beggar and itinerant preacher.

**Bangs, John Kendrick** (1862–1922), a native of New York, was a writer, humorist, editor and satirist.

**Bradstreet, Anne** (1612–1672), was among the most prominent early English poets of North America and the first writer in England's North American colonies to be published.

**Brewer, Ebenezer Cobham** (1810–1897), was born in Edwinstowe, Nottinghamshire. He wrote *A Guide to the Scientific Knowledge of Things Familiar, Brewer's Dictionary of Phrase and Fable* and *The Reader's Handbook.*

**Brontë, Emily Jane** (1818–1848), was an English novelist and poet who is best known for her only novel, *Wuthering Heights,* now considered a classic of English literature.

**Brún, Pádraig de** (1889–1960), also called **Patrick Joseph Monsignor Browne,** was an Irish Catholic priest, linguist, Classicist and Celticist. He was a writer of Irish poetry in the Irish language and the literary translator of many of the greatest works of the Western canon into Modern Irish. He served as President of University College, Galway (UCG), and was known informally as **Paddy Browne.**

**Cary, Alice** (1820–1871), campaigner for women's suffrage and for the abolition of slavery, was born near Cincinnati, Ohio, the older sister of poet Phoebe Cary (1824–1871), with whom she collaborated on several collections of poetry.

**Cooper, George** (1840–1927), was a New Yorker remembered chiefly for his song lyrics, many set to music by Stephen Foster.

**Darley, George** (1795–1846), a native of Dublin, was a poet, novelist, literary critic and author of mathematical texts.

**Dickens, Charles John Huffam** (1812–1870), was an English novelist, journalist, short-story writer and social critic. He created some of literature's best-known fictional characters, and is regarded by many as the greatest novelist of the Victorian era.

**Dodgson, Charles Lutwidge** (1832–1898), better known by his pen name **Lewis Carroll,** was an English author, poet, mathematician, photographer and Anglican priest. His most notable works are *Alice's Adventures in Wonderland* (1865) and *Through the Looking-Glass* (1871).

**Dickinson, Emily Elizabeth** (1830–1886), was an American poet. Little known during her life, she has since become regarded as one of the most important figures in American poetry.

**Dixon, Peter.** English poet and artist.

**Druitt Cole, Charlotte** (1878), Little is known about this British poet, although her work appeared in a number of poetry anthologies for children in the 1920s and 1930s.

**Emerson, Ralph Waldo** (1803–1882), was an American essayist, lecturer, philosopher, abolitionist and poet.

**Frost, Robert Lee** (1874–1963), an American poet who frequently wrote about settings from rural life in New England in the early 20th century. One of his best-known works is *Stopping by Woods on a Snowy Evening.*

**Gales, Winifred Marshall** (1761–1839), was an American novelist and memoirist, born in Newark-upon-Trent, England. She wrote the first novel published by a resident of North Carolina.

**Ghlinn, Áine Ní** is a poet and children's writer with 38 books published. She was Ireland's Laureate na nÓg (Children's Literature Laureate) 2020–23. Awards include Gradam Reics Carló, Children's Book of the Year (on three occasions), KPMG/Children's Books Ireland Fiction Honour Award, Literacy Association of Ireland Book of the Year as well as a range of other awards for poetry, drama and fiction.

**Glúingel, Amergin** (c. 6th century BCE), is a bard and judge for the Milesians in the Irish Mythological Cycle. He was appointed Chief Ollamh of Ireland by his two brothers, the kings of Ireland. A number of poems attributed to Amergin are part of the Milesian mythology.

**Gore-Booth, Eva Selina Laura** (1870–1926), was an Irish poet, theologian and dramatist, and a committed women's suffragist, social worker and labour activist. She was born at Lissadell House, County Sligo, the younger sister of Constance Gore-Booth, later known as the Countess Markievicz.

**Gould, Hannah Flagg** (1789–1865) ,was an American poet. She published several columns of poetry and is best known for her short children's poems. She wrote for and about children because she believed that their innocent spirits were close to God's spirit.

**Gregory, Lady Isabella Augusta** (1852–1932), was an Anglo-Irish dramatist, folklorist and theatre manager and a patron of W.B. Yeats.

**Hall, Eugene J.,** an American poet born in 1849, was known for his vivid and narrative-driven poetry that often depicted scenes of American life and heroism. His work frequently featured themes of nature, rural life and human resilience.

**Hardy, Thomas** (1840–1928), was an English novelist and poet. A Victorian realist in the tradition of George Eliot, he was influenced both in his novels and in his poetry by Romanticism, including the poetry of William Wordsworth.

**Holland, Josiah Gilbert** (1819–1881), was an American novelist, essayist and poet. Born in Western Massachusetts, he was 'the most successful man of letters in the United States' in the latter half of the 19th century, and sold more books in his lifetime than Mark Twain did in his.

**Hyde, Douglas Ross (Dubhghlas de hÍde)** (1860–1949), was an Irish academic, linguist, scholar of the Irish language, politician and diplomat who served as the first president of Ireland from June 1938 to June 1945. He was a leading figure in the Gaelic revival, and was the first president of the Gaelic League, one of the most influential cultural organisations in Ireland at the time.

**Joyce, James Augustine Aloysius** (1882–1941), novelist, poet and literary critic, was a native of Dublin. He is most famous for his novel *Ulysses.*

**Laughton, Freda** (1907–1940s), was born in Bristol but married and settled in County Down. She published just one collection of poems, *A Transitory House* (1945). Her work had already been praised by critics and was starting to appear in anthologies such as Devin A. Garrity's *New Irish Poets* (1948).

**Lawless, Emily** (1845–1913), was an Irish novelist, historian, entomologist, gardener and poet from County Kildare.

**Lawrence, D. H.** (1885–1930) was an influential English writer and poet.

**Ledwidge, Francis Edward** (1887–1917), was born in Slane, County Meath. He was known as the 'poet of the blackbirds', and later as a First World War poet. He was killed in action at Ypres in 1917.

**Le Gallienne, Richard** (1866–1947) was an English poet, essayist, and translator, known for his lyrical and often whimsical style. He was born in Liverpool, England, and educated at Liverpool College before moving to London, where he became part of the literary circles of the time.

**Letts, Winifred Mary** (1882–1972) was an Anglo-Irish writer, born in England to an English father and an Irish mother. She spent much of her life in Ireland, which deeply influenced her writing. Her unmarked grave in Rathcoole was recently rediscovered and a monument unveiled by Michael D. Higgins, President of Ireland.

**Longfellow, Henry Wadsworth** (1807–1882), was an American poet and educator. He was the first American to completely translate Dante Alighieri's *Divine Comedy* and was one of the fireside poets from New England.

**Mac Fheorais, Seán** (1915–1984), was born in County Kildare and worked as a schoolteacher. His lyrical poems appeared in two collections: *Gearrcaigh na hOíche* (1954) and *Léargas – Dánta Fada* (1964).

**MacCarthy, Denis Florence** (1817–1882), poet, translator and biographer, was a native of Dublin.

**MacDonald, George** (1824–1905), was a prolific Scottish author, poet, and Christian minister, widely recognized for his fairy tales, fantasy novels, and theological writings.

**McKay, Festus Claudius (Claude)** (1890–1948), was a Jamaican-American writer and poet. He was a central figure in the Harlem Renaissance.

**McManus, Jean Kyler** (1938–2011) was known for her poems that focus on themes of faith, friendship, love, and personal growth.

**McNally, Sinéad**, is a songwriter, singer, pianist and writer of short stories based in County Louth.

**Mhac an tSaoi, Máire** (1922–2021), was an Irish civil service diplomat, a writer of Modernist poetry in the Corca Dhuibhne dialect of Munster Irish, a memoirist, and a highly important figure within modern literature in Irish.

**Milligan, Terence Alan (Spike)** (1918–2002), was an Irish comedian, writer, musician, poet, playwright and actor.

**Moore, Clement Clarke** (1779–1863), was an American writer, scholar and real estate developer. He is best known for the Christmas poem 'A Visit from St Nicholas', which first named each of Santa Claus's reindeer.

**Moore, Thomas** (1779–1852), also known as Tom Moore, was an Irish writer, poet and lyricist celebrated for his Irish Melodies.

**Newman, St John Henry** (1801–1890), was an English theologian, academic, philosopher, historian, writer, and poet, first as an Anglican priest and later as a Catholic priest and cardinal, who was an important and controversial figure in the religious history of England in the 19th century. He was canonised by the Catholic Church in 2019.

**Ó Raifteirí, Antoine (Anthony Raftery)** (1779–1835), was a blind harpist and Irish-language poet who is often called the last of the wandering bards. He was born in Killedan, near Kiltimagh in County Mayo.

**Ó Ruanaí, Éamonn**, is an Irish writer born in Monaghan.

**O'Keeffe, Adelaide** (1776–1865), was an author and children's poet. A native of Dublin, she was known for her children's poetry and published verse novels for children.

**O'Shaughnessy, Arthur William Edgar** (1844–1881), was a British poet. He was born in London, of Irish descent.

**Pickthall, Marjorie** (1883–1922) was a Canadian poet and writer known for her lyrical and evocative poetry, often reflecting themes of nature, beauty, and spirituality.

**Plunkett, Joseph Mary** (1887–1916), was an Irish republican, poet and journalist. As a leader of the 1916 Easter Rising, he was one of the seven signatories to the Proclamation of the Irish Republic.

**Poe, Edgar Allan** (1809–1849), was an American writer, poet, author, editor and literary critic who is best known for his poetry and short stories, particularly his tales of mystery and the macabre. His grandfather, David Poe, emigrated to America from County Cavan around 1750.

**Posey, Alexander Lawrence** (1873–1908), was an American poet, humorist, journalist and politician in the Creek Nation.

**Potter, Joe**, born in Sussex, England, is a writer, actor and playwright.

**Richardson, Charlotte** (1775–1825), was born in York in England. She published one volume of poetry and two long poems.

**Rittenhouse, Jessie Belle** (1869–1948), a New Yorker, was a literary critic and compiler of anthologies and poetry.

**Roberts, Elizabeth Madox** (1881–1941), was a Kentucky novelist and poet, primarily known for her novels and stories set in central Kentucky's Washington County.

**Russell, George William (A.E.)** (1867–1935) was a prominent figure in the Irish Literary Revival, known for his poetry, essays, and mysticism. His works often explore themes of nature, spirituality, and the beauty of the world.

**Rossetti, Christina Georgina** (1830–1894), was an English writer of romantic, devotional and children's poems, including 'Goblin Market' and 'Remember'.

**Stein, Evaleen** (1863–1923), was an American writer and poet, the author of 11 volumes of stories and three books of verse. An ardent lover of nature, Stein reflected this tendency in most of her poems and stories.

**Stephens, James** (1880–1950), was an Irish novelist and poet, born in Dublin. He was a friend of James Joyce and is an important figure in Irish literature.

**Stevenson, Robert Louis** (1850–1894), was a Scottish novelist, essayist, poet and travel writer. He is best known for works such as *Treasure Island*, *The Strange Case of Dr Jekyll and Mr Hyde*, *Kidnapped* and *A Child's Garden of Verses*.

**Stoddard, Elizabeth Drew** (1823–1902), was an American poet and novelist.

**Swift, Jonathan** (1667–1745), was an Anglo-Irish satirist, author, essayist, political pamphleteer (first for the Whigs, then for the Tories), poet and Anglican cleric who became Dean of St Patrick's Cathedral, Dublin, hence his common sobriquet, 'Dean Swift'. One of his most famous works is *Gulliver's Travels*.

**Taylor, Jane** (1783–1824), was an English poet and novelist best known for the lyrics of the widely known 'Twinkle, Twinkle, Little Star'.

**Teasdale, Sara Trevor** (1884–1933), was an American lyric poet born in St Louis, Missouri. In 1918, she won a Pulitzer Prize for her 1917 poetry collection *Love Songs*.

**Tennyson, Lord Alfred** (1809–1892), was the leading English Victorian poet, and was the Poet Laureate during much of Queen Victoria's reign

**Thayer, Mary Dixon** (1855–1944), was an American poet known primarily for her poem 'Lovely Lady Dressed in Blue', which gained widespread recognition in the mid-20th century.

**Thomas, Philip Edward** (1878–1917) was a British writer of poetry and prose. He started writing poetry at the age of 36, by which time he had already been a prolific critic, biographer, nature writer and travel writer for two decades.

**Tynan, Katharine** (1859–1931), was an Irish writer who is known mainly for her novels and poetry. After her marriage in 1893 to the Trinity College scholar, writer and barrister Henry Albert Hinkson (1865–1919) she usually wrote under the name **Katharine Tynan Hinkson**, or variations thereof.

**Wakeling, Kate**, grew up in Yorkshire and Birmingham. She writes for adults and for children. Her work has been commended in the Forward Prizes for Poetry, awarded the CLiPPA prize for children's poetry and nominated for the Carnegie Medal.

**Walsh, Mary E.** (1864), was an American composer who is best known for 'Black Hawk Waltz' and the hymn 'Bring Flowers of the Fairest'.

**Warner, Susan Bogert** (1819–1885), was an American Presbyterian writer of religious fiction, children's fiction and theological works.

Watts, Isaac (1674–1748), was an English Congregational minister, hymn writer, theologian and logician. He was a prolific and popular hymn writer of some 750 hymns.

Whittier, John Greenleaf (1807–1892), was an American Quaker poet and advocate of the abolition of slavery. He was influenced by the Scottish poet Robert Burns.

Wilde, Oscar Fingal O'Fflahertie Wills (1854–1900), was an Irish poet and playwright. After writing in different forms throughout the 1880s, he became one of the most popular playwrights in London in the early 1890s. He is best remembered for his epigrams and plays, and his novel *The Picture of Dorian Gray*.

Wolfe, Frida, (1869), was a poet whose work is celebrated for its simplicity and charm, known for her contributions to children's poetry.

Wordsworth, William (1770–1850), was an English Romantic poet who, with Samuel Taylor Coleridge, helped to launch the Romantic Age in English literature with their joint publication *Lyrical Ballads* (1798).

Wynne, Annette, was an early 20th-century American poet known for her contributions to children's literature. Her most notable works include the poetry collections *For Days and Days: A Year-Round Treasury of Child Verse*, published in 1919, and *Treasure Things*, published in 1922.

Yeats, William Butler (1865–1939), was an Irish poet, dramatist and writer, and one of the foremost figures of 20th-century literature. He was a driving force behind the Irish Literary Revival and, along with Lady Gregory, founded the Abbey Theatre, serving as its chief during its early years. He was awarded the 1923 Nobel Prize in Literature, and later served two terms as a Senator of the Irish Free State.

# CREDITS • CREIDIÚINTÍ

The publisher gratefully acknowledges the following text copyright holders. All texts are copyright © individual rights holders unless stated otherwise. Every effort has been made to trace copyright holders, or copyright holders not mentioned here. If there have been any errors or omissions, the publisher would be happy to rectify this in any reprint.

| | |
|---|---|
| p17 | Peter Dixon, *Hot Toast*, courtesy of his daughter, Emma Cummins, in loving memory. |
| p22 | Sinéad McNally, *An Ceol*, by kind permission. |
| p30 | Winifred M. Letts, *Saint Brigid*, by kind permission of (her great neice) Oriana Conner. |
| p66 | Sinéad McNally, *Mo Mhadra*, by kind permission. |
| p67 | Otter-Barry Books Ltd for *My Treasures* in *A Dinosaur at the Bus Stop* by Kate Wakeling. |
| p127 | Sinéad McNally, *Samradh*, by kind permission. |
| p135 | Áine Ní Ghlinn, *Eitleog*, by kind permission. |
| p151 | Sinéad McNally, *Gairdín Mhamó*, by kind permission. |
| p165 | Seán Mac Fheorais, *An Gabhar sa Scoil* |
| p173 | Éamonn Ó Ruanaí, *An Grá* |
| p195 | Sinéad McNally, *Nocturnal Nights*, by kind permission. |
| p230 | Winifred M. Letts, *Snowman*, by kind permission of (her great neice) Oriana Conner. |
| p234 | Winifred M. Letts, *Christmas Hearth*, by kind permission of (her great neice) Oriana Conner. |
| p238 | Pádraig de Brún, *Tháinig Long ó Valparaiso* |
| p239 | Spike Milligan, *Granny*, reproduced by permission of Spike Milligan Productions. |
| p235 | Jean Kyler McManus, *The Miracle of Friendship* |
| p241 | Máire Mhac an tSaoi, *Oíche Nollaig*, reproduced by permission of Cló Iar-Chonnacht. |